THE 7-DAY
BASKET

THE 7-DAY BASKET

1 basket. 1 week. 7 meals.
70 delicious recipes to simplify your life

IAN HASTE

DEDICATION

I dedicate this book to my late Mum, Susan, who first taught me the basics of cooking, and to my incredible wife Nicola, for her patience and support throughout the whole process. You – and our beautiful little family – are my absolute rock.

CONTENTS

INTRODUCTION

I've created this book to simplify your weekly shop, save you time, get you creating varied and delicious meals and, in the long run, hopefully save you money. It's apparent that a lot of us like to do 'one shop a week', with the occasional top-ups and sporadic eating out. With this in mind, I've created a book of recipes that will appeal to everyone, from home cooks and uni students who are short on inspiration to busy parents and working professionals who are short on time. This book is based on exactly how I eat.

The 7-Day Basket consists of ten weekly shopping lists that'll provide you with enough ingredients to cook seven tasty and varied meals each week. You can pop to your local supermarket with these pre-written shopping lists or order online and get everything you need delivered straight to your door. The book is designed to suit your lifestyle, so feel free to eat the meals in the evening or take them to work and have them for your lunch. Either way, it will reduce the amount of time you spend worrying over what to cook and give you delicious recipes that you'll want to eat.

Each recipe is designed to cater for two people, but I want the book to suit you and your needs, so please halve the ingredients if you're eating on your own, or multiply to suit your circumstances.

The 7-Day Basket will guide any home cook to create tasty, quick and balanced dishes whatever the season. Choose the start or end of the book for those winter warmer menus, or if it's sunny and you fancy a lighter week, head to the centre where you'll find lots of fresh summer dishes. Whichever basket you choose to cook from, I have included a balanced mix of recipes, so you'll find Mondays are meat free and I always end the week with a Sunday classic, sometimes with a twist.

To shop and cook in *The 7-Day Basket* way, remember: the freezer is your friend. Make sure you freeze any meat, chicken or fish in advance to maintain its freshness if you are cooking it later in the week. And feel free to cook the meals in whichever order suits you. I have also made some of the recipes into bigger portions as I love batch cooking. This gives you some extras for lunch the next day or leftovers to put in the freezer for those lazy days – ultimately saving you time and money.

With my background as a gastro pub chef, I wanted to share my recipes in a different way and to a broader audience. So, for the past four years I've hosted a YouTube channel under the name of *Haste's Kitchen*, where I create and present recipes. Eating healthily and balanced has never been so easy, and my ethos is all about staying fit and simplifying nutritious, balanced recipes so we can all eat mouthwatering, tasty meals.

This book will hopefully cut down the time you spend dawdling in supermarket aisles. It's my ambition to turn this simple and cost-effective way of cooking into your new tradition, ensuring you enjoy delicious meals every night of the week!

Ian

CUPBOARD STAPLES

This book is separated into a weekly format, with varied weeks throughout and a total of 70 recipes. Every basket starts with your menu plan and a specially prepared shopping list for the week ahead. The list has been carefully separated into aisles, with ingredients to buy listed under Meat & Fish, Dairy & Eggs, Vegetables, Herbs, Fruit, General and, lastly, the Cupboard Staples. This should make your food shop much easier!

For the cupboard stuff, I've listed what I think are general store cupboard regulars, many of which you will probably already have at home. However, do make sure to check your cupboards before going shopping or clicking online. If you are short of anything on this list, please remember to get the staples stocked up.

With fresh ingredients being bought at the start of the week, think ahead when buying your food. I always search to the bottom of the piles or shelves to ensure the longest shelf life. Also, get anything into the freezer which you want to stay fresh for later in the week, especially fish, meat and chicken. Remember the freezer is your friend for food preparation and especially for those all-important leftovers. Just defrost for 4–6 hours or the night before the chosen recipe day.

Lastly, remember to check the Spices & Making Your Own Blends section on pages 14–15 to start building up your own flavour drawer at home. If you fancy changing any of the weeks' recipes, you will then have your own spice mixes to make up and enjoy.

CUPBOARD STAPLES

DAIRY
butter

BAKING
baking powder
brown sugar
honey
light spelt or plain flour
salt and pepper
sea salt
self-raising flour
sugar

GENERAL
balsamic glaze
basmati rice
Dijon mustard
gravy granules
mayonnaise
spaghetti
tomato ketchup
tomato paste
vegetable, chicken and beef
stock pots/cubes

HERBS & SPICES
bay leaves
cayenne pepper
chilli flakes
chilli powder
cinnamon sticks
cloves
coriander powder
coriander seeds
cumin powder
cumin seeds
curry powder
dried oregano
fenugreek seeds
garam masala
ground ginger
paprika
smoked paprika
turmeric

OILS & VINEGARS
balsamic vinegar
olive oil
rice wine vinegar
sesame oil
sunflower oil
vegetable oil
white wine vinegar

SAUCES
dark soy sauce
fish sauce
oyster sauce
soy sauce
Worcestershire sauce

'THIS BOOK IS BASED ON EXACTLY HOW MY WIFE AND I PLAN, SHOP AND EAT; COMBINING FITNESS WITH A BALANCED DIET.'

SPICES & MAKING YOUR OWN BLENDS

If you're new to them, spices can be intimidating, especially if you're unsure of quantities or what culinary results they will achieve. Here, I break down the different variations and why they're so important for so many cuisines.

Throughout this book you'll start to understand the flavours of spices, learning their unique properties, so that in no time at all you'll know how to flavour any meal with any kind of spice. So, clear out a drawer or cupboard in the kitchen and let's start building your very own flavour hub.

When looking at spices, think of them as *enhancers*. When a musician is writing a song, they'll look at all the variations to fill the sound – bass lines, trebles, etc. – and herbs and spices, for a chef or a home cook, work in exactly the same way. Spices can tweak bland recipes by building up layers of tastes and textures, and they can also bring vibrant colours to a dish.

When you eat Middle Eastern, Thai or Indian food, you may have noticed that many of the dishes have a deep yellow, orange or red colour. This is because of the spices used, such as saffron, turmeric, chilli and paprika, which give intense colour, making dishes brighter and more appealing.

Try thinking of all the tastes spices can achieve as well as the heat, the sweetness, the colour and smells, and, after all, aroma is what you want in the kitchen. Yes, salt and pepper are the standard seasonings that might first come to mind, but there are a whole host of other spices that bring out the natural flavours of food and are just waiting to be discovered.

Think:

T — **TASTE**
A — **ADD**
S — **SEASON**
T — **TASTE**
E — **EAT**

With the huge variety of spices and how easily accessible they've become, I recommend adding one to two per week to your food shop. This way you'll start to build a library of different varieties. Don't be scared by how many there are, just build your collection slowly. I promise you, having these in the cupboard gives you the flexibility to make anything.

Along with stand-alone spices, there are also blends and rubs made from mixing spices together. So, along with the basics opposite, I've created a set of spice rubs, which you can easily mix together to vary my recipes or keep in flavour jars for impromptu barbecues and simple suppers. Each of the spice rubs makes enough to cover two portions of chicken, salmon steaks, pork cubes, beef or lamb steaks or halloumi, mushrooms, peppers, tofu and aubergine.

BASICS

bay leaves
caraway seeds
cardamom pods
cayenne pepper
chilli flakes
chilli powder
chipotle seeds
cinnamon sticks
cloves
cumin powder
cumin seeds
curry powder
dried basil
dried coriander
dried lemongrass
dried mint
dried oregano
dried rosemary
dried sage
dried tarragon
dried thyme
fennel seeds
garam masala
garlic powder
ground allspice
ground cinnamon
ground ginger
ground mace
ground nutmeg
kaffir lime leaves
mustard seeds
nigella seeds
onion powder
paprika
saffron
smoked paprika
star anise
sumac
turmeric

PERI PERI RUB

*Spicy chilli sauce –
especially good on chicken*
pinch of salt
½ tsp paprika
½ tsp ground cinnamon
½ tsp garlic powder
½ tsp dried oregano
2 cardamoms, seeds ground
½ tsp hot chilli flakes
½ tsp sugar
½ tsp ground ginger

TANDOORI SPICE MIX

Subtle Indian spice mix
¼ tsp garlic powder
½ tsp ground ginger
2 cloves, ground
¼ tsp ground nutmeg
1 tsp cumin powder
1 tsp coriander powder
½ tsp fennel seeds
1 tsp chilli powder
½ tsp black pepper

THAI 7-SPICE

*Lovely punchy
Thai flavours*
¼ tsp ground ginger
¼ tsp chilli flakes
¼ tsp cumin powder
pinch of salt
¼ tsp chilli powder
¼ tsp garlic powder
½ tsp coriander powder
juice of ½ lemon
¼ tsp ground cinnamon
1 ground star anise
pinch of white pepper
2 kaffir lime leaves, ground

FAJITA MIX

*The perfect
Mexican-style blend*
½ tsp chilli powder
pinch of salt
1 tsp paprika
½ tsp sugar
½ tsp onion powder
½ tsp garlic powder
1 tsp cayenne pepper
1 tsp cumin powder

RAS-EL-HANOUT

Moroccan-style spices
¼ tsp black pepper
1 tsp coriander powder
1 tsp ground ginger
½ tsp smoked paprika
½ tsp allspice
1 tsp ground cardamom
½ tsp mace
¼ tsp ground nutmeg
½ tsp turmeric
½ tsp cayenne pepper
1 tsp ground cloves

HARISSA BLEND

*North African
spicy seasoning*
¼ tsp garlic powder
pinch of salt
½ tsp cumin powder
½ tsp chilli powder
½ tsp coriander powder
½ tsp garlic powder
½ tsp dried mint
½ tsp caraway seeds
½ tsp cayenne pepper

15

SERVES
2

EACH RECIPE SERVES TWO PEOPLE.
HOWEVER, THEY HAVE BEEN CREATED
TO BE EASY TO HALVE AND MAKE FOR
ONE OR JUST MULTIPLY THE INGREDIENTS
AND EXTEND THE COOKING TIME, IF YOU
NEED TO, IF YOU'RE FEEDING A CROWD.

BASKET

1

WARMING

THIS IS THE PERFECT WINTER WARMER WEEK. WHEN IT'S COLD, WET AND DARK OUTSIDE, GET CRACKING WITH THIS BASKET! THE LASAGNE AND CASSOULET RECIPES IN THIS WEEK MAKE AMPLE PORTIONS, GREAT FOR LEFTOVERS TO TAKE TO WORK FOR LUNCH.

MENU FOR THE WEEK AHEAD

MONDAY
Vegetarian Bucatini all'Amatriciana

TUESDAY
Bavette Steak with Shiitake, Kale
& Thrice-Cooked Chips

WEDNESDAY
Yakisoba Pork Noodles

THURSDAY
Teriyaki Salmon

FRIDAY
Shredded Chicken & Stilton Lasagne
with Buttered Kale

SATURDAY
King Prawn & Pineapple Red Curry

SUNDAY
Toulouse Sausage Cassoulet with Charred Cabbage

SHOPPING LIST FOR THE WEEK AHEAD

BASKET

MEAT & FISH

2 bavette steaks or
  skirt or rib-eye
4 chicken breasts
200g frozen/raw
  king prawns
2 x 250g pork chops
  (without bones)
2 x 120g salmon
  fillets
125g smoked pancetta
6–8 Toulouse sausages

DAIRY & EGGS

200g blue cheese
400ml double cream
150g mozzarella cheese
2 tablespoons grated
  Parmesan cheese

VEGETABLES

1 carrot
300g chestnut
  mushrooms
9 garlic cloves
1½ teaspoons
  grated ginger
200g kale
100g mangetout
125g mushrooms
4 onions
2 large potatoes,
  such as Maris Piper
1 Savoy cabbage
2 shallots

200g spinach
5 spring onions

HERBS

12 sprigs of coriander
2 sprigs of parsley
10 sprigs of thyme

FRUIT

3 limes
120g pack of pineapple

GENERAL

1 bread roll
200g bucatini pasta
3 x 400g tins of
  chopped tomatoes
400ml tin of coconut milk
25g dried shiitake
  mushrooms
410g tin of haricot beans
12 lasagne sheets
2 tablespoons red
  curry paste
275ml red wine
4 teaspoons sesame seeds
250g soba noodles
200ml white wine

CUPBOARD

basmati rice
butter
chilli flakes
fish sauce
honey
light spelt flour
olive oil
oyster sauce
rice wine vinegar
salt and pepper
sea salt
smoked paprika
soy sauce
tomato ketchup
tomato paste
vegetable oil
Worcestershire sauce

VEGETARIAN BUCATINI ALL'AMATRICIANA

Cooking time: 20 minutes
Difficulty: Easy

Historically made with cured pork jowl, I've turned this into a beautiful vegetarian version using smoky paprika and mushrooms to give that lovely rich flavour to the sauce.

1 tablespoon olive oil
1 onion, peeled and finely sliced
1 garlic clove, peeled and crushed
125g mushrooms, finely sliced
1½ teaspoons smoked paprika
200g bucatini pasta
400g tin of chopped tomatoes
½ teaspoon chilli flakes
2 sprigs of parsley,
    finely chopped
2 tablespoons grated
    Parmesan cheese
salt and pepper

Pour the oil into a hot pan, add the onion, garlic and mushrooms and cook until beginning to soften, then add the smoked paprika and cook for 3–4 minutes.

Add the pasta to a pan of salted boiling water and cook for 7–8 minutes, then drain.

Meanwhile, add the tomatoes to the onion and mushrooms and season with salt, pepper and the chilli flakes. Once bubbling and beginning to thicken, stir the pasta into the sauce.

Scatter in the parsley and serve, twisting the pasta onto the plates with a tablespoon of Parmesan sprinkled over each.

BAVETTE STEAK WITH SHIITAKE, KALE & THRICE-COOKED CHIPS

Cooking time: 45 minutes
Chilling time: 30 minutes
Difficulty: Hard

Bavette steak is one of my favourite steaks, cooked here medium-rare, with the combination of crunch from the thrice-cooked chips and the smooth shiitake flavours infusing the kale. This has to be my favourite steak night recipe.

---

2 large potatoes, such as
    Maris Piper, peeled
2 bavette steaks or skirt
    (rib-eye is also good)
450ml vegetable oil
1 teaspoon salt
1 teaspoon pepper
2 teaspoons olive oil
25g butter
2 garlic cloves, peeled and
    1 whole and 1 crushed
2 sprigs of thyme
5g dried shiitake mushrooms,
    soaked in hot water
2 shallots, peeled and
    finely chopped
150ml red wine
100g kale
2 teaspoons honey
sea salt, for the chips

Bring a pan of salted water to the boil. Rinse the potatoes to clean off some of the starch, then slice into large, chunky-size chips and boil for about 4 minutes until they slide off a knife, making sure they don't overcook so they retain their shape.

Drain the chips and chill in the fridge for about 20–30 minutes. Take the steaks out of the fridge and allow to come up to room temperature.

Heat all but 1 teaspoon of the vegetable oil up to 140°C (285°F) in a fryer, add the chips and cook in small batches for around 6–7 minutes until they start getting slightly crunchy, but still have no colour. Take out and add to a draining tray. Turn the heat up on the fryer to 180°C (350°F) for later.

Season the steaks on both sides with the salt, pepper and olive oil. Heat a griddle or frying pan to piping hot and lay the steaks down, sear on all sides for 1 minute, then add the butter, whole garlic (sliced in half) and the thyme sprigs and baste the steaks, turning them on all sides for around 3–5 minutes to create a brown crust. Take the steaks out to rest. Keep the juices and colouring in the pan for cooking the kale.

→

Bavette Steak / continued

Add the chips to the 180°C (350°F) oil and cook in batches again for about 3–4 minutes or until coloured golden brown and extra crunchy.

Meanwhile, in the steak pan, add a splash of the mushroom water, the shallots, crushed garlic and the wine in small splashes, reducing the sauce as it cooks. Add the kale and finely chop the mushrooms and add along with the honey. Pour in splashes of the mushroom water until the kale is steamed and the sauce is dark and reduced. There shouldn't be too much sauce – you only need a little as it's very strong in flavour.

Drain the chips and season with sea salt. Serve the kale with the sliced steak on top alongside the thrice-cooked chips.

YAKISOBA PORK NOODLES

Cooking time: 15 minutes
Difficulty: Easy

Yakisoba is an amazing fried noodle dish from the streets of Japan. You can add any meat, fish or veg to this and get the same delicious results. Perfect for when you are in need of a quick dish in the middle of the week.

2 teaspoons honey

1 tablespoon tomato ketchup

3 tablespoons oyster sauce

1 garlic clove, peeled and crushed

1 tablespoon soy sauce

2 tablespoons Worcestershire
    sauce

1 teaspoon peeled and
    grated ginger

3 tablespoons vegetable oil

1 onion, peeled and finely sliced

2 x 250g pork chops (without
    bones), finely cut into slithers

10g dried shiitake mushrooms,
    soaked in hot water,
    roughly chopped

250g soba noodles

1 carrot, peeled and sliced
    into matchsticks

3 spring onions, trimmed and finely
    sliced (use the tops too)

3 cabbage leaves, finely shredded

2 teaspoons sesame seeds

lime wedges, for squeezing

Add the honey, ketchup, oyster sauce, garlic, soy sauce, Worcestershire sauce and ginger to a bowl and mix together.

In a frying pan or wok, heat the oil until beginning to smoke, then add the onion, pork and mushrooms and cook for 2 minutes until the onion begins to soften and the pork firms up.

Cook the noodles in a saucepan of boiling water until they begin to soften but still have a bit of bite.

Now add the noodles to the frying pan along with the carrot, spring onion and cabbage, and continue to fry for another minute.

Pour in the sauce in small amounts, adding until you have your desired amount of flavour. I like the whole lot, but some might like only a light flavouring.

To serve, add the noodles to a plate with a scattering of sesame seeds and the wedges of lime for squeezing over.

TERIYAKI SALMON

Cooking time: 20 minutes
Difficulty: Easy

This sticky-sweet glaze works perfectly with most meats and fish – the caramelisation on the crust is what's key to its success. Pair with crunchy veg and soft fluffy rice for the perfect 20-minute meal.

2 teaspoons honey

2 tablespoons soy sauce

1 garlic clove, peeled and crushed

2 sprigs of thyme

½ teaspoon peeled and
grated ginger

1 tablespoon rice wine vinegar

2 teaspoons sesame seeds

4 sprigs of coriander, leaves only

300g (1½ cups) basmati rice

750ml (3 cups) water

2 x 120g salmon fillets

100g mangetout, sliced

2 spring onions, trimmed and
finely sliced diagonally

Mix the honey, soy sauce, garlic, thyme, ginger, vinegar, half the sesame seeds and the coriander leaves together in a bowl.

Meanwhile, add the rice with double the amount of water to a pan and bring to the boil. Once boiling, cook for 3 minutes, turn off the heat and put a lid on the pan so the rice can carry on steaming for 7–8 minutes. Do not stir as you want the rice to steam, absorb the water and fluff up.

Score the salmon skin with light lines. To a hot pan, add the fish skin-side down and keep at a high heat. After 2 minutes, flip the fish over and add half the sauce. Keep dousing the fish with the sauce, then add the rest of the sauce and keep cooking until you have a sticky glaze, almost like a caramel sauce.

Take out the fish, add a splash of water to the pan with the mangetout and cook for 30 seconds.

Serve the rice with the mangetout and the fish over the top. Drizzle over any of the leftover sauce and finish with a sprinkle of spring onion and the remaining sesame seeds.

SHREDDED CHICKEN & STILTON LASAGNE WITH BUTTERED KALE

Cooking time: 40 minutes
Difficulty: Moderate

This is a great twist on the classic lasagne – a big meal that will leave you with plenty of delicious leftovers for next day's lunch or even the freezer. The creamy wine and cheese sauce with the mozzarella topping are what make this dish special. You can swap the kale for any greens if preferred.

50g butter

1 onion, peeled and finely chopped

2 garlic cloves, peeled and crushed

4 chicken breasts, sliced into
  thin strips

300g chestnut mushrooms,
  finely chopped

1 tablespoon light spelt flour

200ml white wine

400ml double cream

200g blue cheese

200g spinach

3 sprigs of thyme

12 lasagne sheets

150g mozzarella cheese, grated

100g kale

salt and pepper

Preheat the oven to 180°C/160°C fan/gas 4.

Add half the butter to a hot pan with the onion, garlic and chicken and cook for 4–5 minutes until the onion is turning in colour. Add the mushrooms and cook for 2 minutes, then add the flour (this will stick to the chicken), wine and cream and mix well, making sure there are no lumps. Crumble in the blue cheese, stir to melt in, then add the spinach. Drag your hand down two of the thyme sprigs and stir the leaves into the sauce until the spinach has wilted.

Add a thin layer of sauce to a rectangular dish and top with a layer of lasagne, then more sauce. Continue the layers until you reach the top of the dish, finishing with lasagne sheets and just a small amount of sauce on top. Sprinkle with the mozzarella and leaves from the last sprig of thyme.

Bake the lasagne for 25 minutes or until bubbling on top and the cheese is crusting.

About 8 minutes from the end of the cooking time, add the kale to a small amount of water along with the remaining butter. Season, cover with a lid and steam for 5–6 minutes. Serve with the lasagne.

KING PRAWN & PINEAPPLE RED CURRY

Cooking time: 20 minutes
Difficulty: Easy

Thai flavours and sweet-and-sour ingredients make this dish. Curries don't need to be complicated, instead concentrate on simple fresh ingredients, which will come together to make the perfect spicy dish. Add red chilli if you want more punch.

300g (1½ cups) basmati rice
750ml (3 cups) water
400ml tin of coconut milk
120g pack of pineapple
1 tablespoon fish sauce
1 lime, plus extra wedges,
   for serving
2 tablespoons red curry paste
8 sprigs of coriander
100g mangetout
200g frozen/raw king prawns,
   defrosted, cleaned and deveined

Add the rice with double the amount of water to a pan and bring to the boil. Once boiling, cook for 3 minutes, turn off the heat and put a lid on the pan so the rice can carry on steaming for 7–8 minutes. Do not stir as you want the rice to steam, absorb the water and fluff up.

Whilst this is cooking, add the coconut milk, pineapple and fish sauce to a separate pan and bring to a simmer. Cut the lime in half, squeeze in the juice, then add the lime halves and stir in the curry paste.

Take half the sprigs of coriander and cut into tiny bits, rocking the knife over the top of them to make them into almost a paste (use a blender with a dash of water if you can't chop enough). Stir into the sauce. Chop the mangetout into halves and add to the sauce along with the prawns and cook for a further minute or two.

Serve the curry over the rice with a scattering of the remaining chopped coriander and lime wedges.

TOULOUSE SAUSAGE CASSOULET WITH CHARRED CABBAGE

Cooking time: 50 minutes
Difficulty: Moderate

The rich sauce and garlicky sausages in this simple-to-make recipe pair perfectly with the charred cabbage. This is the dish I'd save for a Sunday lunch or a colder day. Warning: you don't have to eat all of this – it's great for lunch the next day as the servings are large!

25g butter
1 onion, peeled and chopped
6–8 Toulouse sausages
125g smoked pancetta, chopped
2 garlic cloves, peeled and crushed
1½ tablespoons tomato paste
10g dried shiitake mushrooms,
    soaked in hot water
125ml red wine
2 x 400g tins of chopped tomatoes
410g tin of haricot beans, drained
    and rinsed
1 tablespoon honey
3 sprigs of thyme
1 bread roll, blitzed to breadcrumbs
1 Savoy cabbage, cut into quarters,
    (set aside 3 leaves for the
    Yakisoba Pork Noodles, page 31)
1 tablespoon vegetable oil
salt and pepper

Preheat the oven to 180°C/160°C fan/gas 4.

Add the butter, onion, sausages, pancetta and garlic to an ovenproof hot pan and cook over a medium heat until the onion softens and the sausages are browned. Add the tomato paste and cook for about a minute or two more, then add the drained mushrooms and wine and simmer again for a further 2–3 minutes. Season and add the tomatoes, haricot beans, honey and thyme. Leave with a lid on to cook for about 15 minutes, then take off the lid and sprinkle with the breadcrumbs.

Bake the cassoulet for 15–18 minutes until the sauce is thick and the breadcrumbs golden.

Meanwhile, rub the cabbage with the oil and add to a piping hot griddle pan. Cook on both sides undisturbed for 3 minutes each side. They will char and burn slightly, but don't panic. Add salt and pepper to season before serving the cabbage with lashings of the crunchy-topped cassoulet.

BASKET

2

ROUND THE WORLD

....

WHEN YOU WANT A VARIED WEEK,
THIS IS DEFINITELY THE BASKET!
MOROCCAN, ITALIAN, INDONESIAN AND
A THAI-INSPIRED FRENCH PAPILLOTE
RECIPE ALL FEATURE IN THIS ONE.

....

MENU FOR THE WEEK AHEAD

MONDAY
Zaalouk, Spiced Honey & Pistachio
Couscous with Flat Breads

TUESDAY
Zesty Seared Tuna Steak with Spinach & Avocado

WEDNESDAY
King Prawn Nasi Goreng Fried Rice

THURSDAY
Salmon & Grapefruit en Papillote
with Soft-Boiled Eggs

FRIDAY
My BLT Pizzas

SATURDAY
Slow-Cooked Beef Rendang

SUNDAY
Spatchcock Chicken & Cavolo Nero
Bake with Roast Garlic Mash

SHOPPING LIST FOR THE WEEK AHEAD

BASKET

MEAT & FISH

500g beef stewing
   steak
1 small chicken
300g frozen/raw
   king prawns
70g Parma ham
2 x 120g salmon steaks
2 x 120g tuna steaks

DAIRY & EGGS

4 eggs
70ml milk
1 mozzarella ball
4 tablespoons yogurt

VEGETABLES

1 aubergine
200g baby spinach
1 carrot
300g cavolo nero
150g chestnut
   mushrooms
¾ cucumber
1 garlic bulb, plus
   9 garlic cloves
2cm piece of ginger, plus
   1½ teaspoons grated
2 green chillies
2 onions
2 large potatoes
6 red chillies
1 red onion
60g rocket
6 spring onions

HERBS

10 basil leaves
13 sprigs of coriander
5 kaffir lime leaves
1 lemongrass stalk
2 sprigs of mint

FRUIT

1 avocado
1 grapefruit
3 limes
6 tomatoes, 4 large

GENERAL

4 cardamom pods
2 x 400ml tins of
   coconut milk
370g couscous
6 dried apricots
½ teaspoon instant yeast
1 small handful
   of pistachios
3 strands of saffron
2 teaspoons crushed
   salted peanuts
2 tablespoons sriracha
   sauce
3 star anise
4 teaspoons
   tamarind paste

CUPBOARD

basmati rice
brown sugar
butter
cinnamon sticks
cumin powder
dark soy sauce
honey
light spelt flour
olive oil
paprika
salt and pepper
soy sauce
sugar
tomato paste
vegetable oil

ZAALOUK, SPICED HONEY & PISTACHIO COUSCOUS WITH FLAT BREADS

Cooking time: 40 minutes
Difficulty: Hard

This one takes a little bit of effort, but the effort is worth taking. You'll end up with this beautiful vegetarian Moroccan salad with layers of sticky pistachio and apricot-infused couscous, perfect scooped up with the easy-to-make flat breads.

Flat breads
250g light spelt flour
1½ tablespoons olive oil
100ml water
salt and pepper

Zaalouk
1 tablespoon olive oil, plus
    extra to serve
1 aubergine, stalk removed, diced
1½ teaspoons tomato paste
2 garlic cloves, peeled and minced
4 large tomatoes, finely chopped
1½ teaspoons cumin powder
1 teaspoon paprika
3 sprigs of coriander, leaves only

Couscous
370g couscous
350ml water
1 cinnamon stick
3 strands of saffron
1 small handful of
    deshelled pistachios
6 dried apricots, roughly chopped
½ tablespoon olive oil
1 tablespoon honey
4 tablespoons yogurt

To make the bread dough, mix the flour and 1½ teaspoons salt in a bowl. Create a well in the middle and, using a spoon, mix in the oil, then add the water a little at a time, mixing well. You can use your hands or a spoon to bring it together until it forms a ball – you want the sides of the bowl to become clean. Once you have a dough consistency, stretch it out in the bowl, then knead for 5 minutes. Wrap the ball of dough in cling film and set aside.

Pour the oil into a heated frying pan, add the aubergine, season and cook for about 10 minutes until really soft – you want the consistency to be falling apart and almost mushy. Add the tomato paste and cook for 2 minutes, then add the garlic, tomatoes, cumin and paprika. I use a potato masher to squash everything down (the back of a fork will also work), then cook for 5 minutes until it thickens.

Add the couscous, water, the cinnamon stick and saffron to a second pan, season and bring to the boil, then cover with a lid and reduce the heat.

In a third small saucepan, add the pistachios, apricots and oil, cook for 1–2 minutes, then add the honey and cook for 1 minute until sticky and

$\rightarrow$

46

Zaalouk / continued

caramel-glazed. You don't want it to stick and burn, so keep an eye on it! The couscous should now be cooked and fluffy and have absorbed all the water.

Unwrap the bread dough, roll into a cylinder shape and cut into four portions. Roll each portion out on a lightly floured work surface into a thin bread about the size of a regular plate. Heat a frying pan until piping hot. Add a bread, leaving until it starts to bubble and char slightly, then flip over. In around 30–50 seconds the flat bread should start to separate as it fills with air. Remove to a plate and repeat with the remaining portions of dough.

To serve, add the zaalouk to a sharing bowl with a glug of oil and a scattering of coriander leaves, then to another bowl add the couscous and top with the sticky apricots and pistachios. Tear the breads, add some zaalouk along with the topped couscous and then a spoon of the yogurt also topped with a glug of olive oil.

ZESTY SEARED TUNA STEAK WITH SPINACH & AVOCADO

Cooking time: 10 minutes
Marinating time: 20 minutes
Difficulty: Easy

This Asian-flavoured tuna steak, seared rare with wilted spinach and creamy avocado, is the perfect lighter meal for the week.

2 x 120g tuna steaks

2 garlic cloves, peeled and crushed

1 teaspoon peeled and
  grated ginger

2 teaspoons soy sauce

1 teaspoon brown sugar

200g baby spinach

8 sprigs of coriander, chopped

1 avocado, halved, stoned
  and thinly sliced

Add the tuna steaks to a bowl along with the garlic, ginger, soy sauce and brown sugar and marinate for 15–20 minutes.

Heat a griddle pan until smoking hot, add the tuna steaks and sear on each side for 40 seconds for rare and 1 minute on each side for pink (these are the best ways to cook the tuna for this recipe).

Remove the tuna from the pan and put to one side. Add the spinach to the pan with a splash of the marinade and wilt for 1 minute. Again, place to one side. Now add the rest of the marinade to the same pan along with the coriander, and cook for 2 minutes until the sauce starts to caramelise.

Serve each portion of the spinach with half the avocado and a sliced tuna steak and top with the coriander reduction.

KING PRAWN NASI GORENG FRIED RICE

Cooking time: 30 minutes
Difficulty: Moderate

Nasi goreng 'fried rice' is one of those dishes that is very simple to make, yet packs in so many interesting textures and flavours. In Indonesia you find lots of variations, with it often being eaten with lots of chilli sauce for a spicy breakfast.

200g (1 cup) basmati rice

500ml (2 cups) water

2½ tablespoons vegetable oil

1 onion, peeled and finely sliced

2 teaspoons tamarind paste

2 garlic cloves, peeled and crushed

1 red chilli

2 teaspoons brown sugar

juice of 1 lime

300g frozen/raw king prawns, defrosted, cleaned and deveined

1 carrot, peeled and sliced into matchsticks

2 tablespoons dark soy sauce

80g cavolo nero, shredded

2 eggs

2 teaspoons crushed salted peanuts

2 spring onions, trimmed and sliced into thin matchsticks

¼ cucumber, sliced into thin matchsticks

2 tablespoons sriracha sauce

Add the rice with double the amount of water to a pan and bring to the boil. Once boiling, cook for 3 minutes, turn off the heat and put a lid on the pan so the rice can carry on steaming for 7–8 minutes. Do not stir as you want the rice to steam, absorb the water and fluff up.

Meanwhile, add 1 tablespoon of the oil to a hot pan and cook half the onion for around 15 minutes until dark and crispy. Leave on paper towels to dry.

Add the tamarind paste, garlic, red chilli, brown sugar, the remaining onion and half the lime juice to a food processor and blitz to a paste. Add 1 tablespoon vegetable oil to a large pan or wok, then add the paste and cook for 30 seconds over a high heat. Add the king prawns, carrot, soy sauce and cabbage. Cook for 30 seconds, then add the rice, stir together and cook for around 1 minute at full heat until piping hot and the prawns are pink.

Fry the eggs in a second pan using the remaining oil. Serve by spooning the rice mix into a bowl, then tipping the bowl upside down onto a plate to give you a dome of rice. Top with the eggs, nuts, crispy onions, spring onion, cucumber and a squirt of sriracha sauce.

SALMON & GRAPEFRUIT EN PAPILLOTE WITH SOFT-BOILED EGGS

Cooking time: 25 minutes
Difficulty: Easy

The presentation of this simple little dish is the impressive bit – there's something about serving up small steam-filled parcels and popping them open to reveal the perfectly cooked fish inside. Top with a soft-boiled egg, which works so well with the fish.

2 x 120g salmon steaks
1 garlic clove, peeled and crushed
½ teaspoon peeled and
    grated ginger
1 red chilli, finely chopped
220g cavolo nero,
    roughly chopped
2 sprigs of coriander, leaves only
4 spring onions, trimmed and
    finely sliced at an angle
squeeze of lime juice
2 eggs
½ cucumber
1 grapefruit, segmented
2 teaspoons olive oil
2 sprigs of mint, leaves only
salt and pepper

Preheat the oven to 180°C/160°C fan/gas 4.

Lay out two sheets of baking paper around the size of an A3 sheet each.

To the centre of both, add the fish, garlic, ginger, chilli, cavolo nero, half the coriander, the spring onion and a squeeze of lime. Fold the paper over to seal the fish inside. Add a little water and seal the sides. Put the parcels on a baking tray and bake for 15 minutes.

Add the eggs to a small pan of boiling water and cook for 5 minutes. Take out, cool, peel and halve.

Using a potato peeler, ribbon the cucumber into small slithers.

Add the grapefruit, cucumber, olive oil, mint leaves and the rest of the coriander to a bowl, mix and season. Arrange this mix on two plates, then add the papillotes and cut open to release the steam. Serve with the soft-boiled eggs on top.

MY BLT PIZZAS

Cooking time: 30 minutes
Proving time: 20 minutes
Difficulty: Moderate

Who doesn't love a BLT? Here's my version of this perfect flavour combination, all prepped up on a crispy, doughy pizza. Remember to get the dough made in advance.

Pizza

175g light spelt flour
pinch of sugar
½ teaspoon salt
½ teaspoon instant yeast
120ml warm water
½ tablespoon olive oil

Sauce and toppings

1 tablespoon olive oil, plus
   extra for drizzling
2 tablespoons tomato paste
2 tomatoes, finely chopped,
   1 for sauce and 1 for topping ·
1 teaspoon paprika
10 basil leaves, 2 leaves finely
   sliced, 8 torn
1 small red onion, peeled and thinly
   sliced into long slithers
70g Parma ham, torn
1 mozzarella ball
60g rocket
salt and pepper

Preheat the oven to 190°C/170°C fan/gas 5.

Thoroughly mix the flour, sugar and salt in a bowl, then stir the yeast into the water. Make a well in the flour and add the water a little at a time, bringing to a dough with a spoon or by hand. Stretch the dough for 5 minutes until elastic and cleaned away from the sides of the bowl. Add the oil, tip onto a flour-covered surface, then stretch away from you and knead for 4 minutes. Cover with a cloth and set aside in a warm place for 20 minutes.

Heat the oil and tomato paste in a small pan for a minute. Add one of the tomatoes and the paprika and season. Add the finely sliced basil and cook for a minute until thicker and spreadable for the bases.

Now for the fun bit: pizza-making time! Roll the dough into a ball on a flour-dusted surface and cut into two. Roll out both balls to your desired pizza size: large for a thinner, crispy base or small for a deep-pan doughy pizza. Scoop some tomato mix onto the centre of each pizza and, using the back of a spoon and circular motions, spread all the way to around an inch back from the crust edge.

Scatter over the onion, torn basil, remaining tomato and Parma ham and season, then shred the mozzarella over. Bake for 15–20 minutes to your desired colour (20 minutes for a crusty edge). Serve with a topping of rocket and drizzle of olive oil.

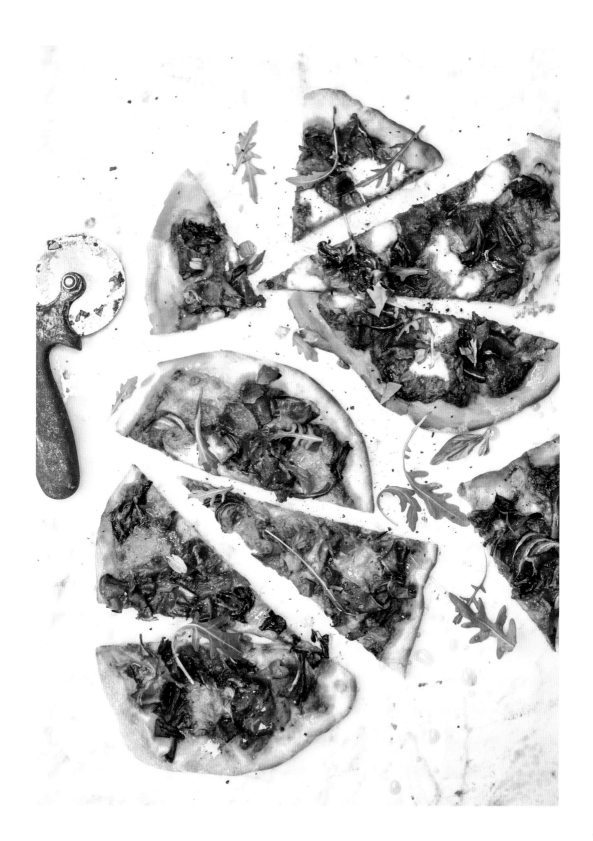

SLOW-COOKED BEEF RENDANG

Cooking time: 2 hours
Difficulty: Moderate

This dry curry works really well when made in a slow cooker, or simply make the paste, add everything to a saucepan and relax whilst it creates this insanely good, flavour-packed beef rendang. It takes some time, but the resulting flavours are out of this world, so be patient!

1 onion, peeled

2 garlic cloves, peeled

2cm piece of ginger, peeled

8 sprigs of coriander

4 cardamom pods, crushed
  and seeds removed

1 lemongrass stalk

2 red chillies

2 teaspoons tamarind paste

3 tablespoons vegetable oil

2 tablespoons brown sugar

500g beef stewing steak,
  cut into cubes

1 cinnamon stick

3 star anise

2 x 400ml tins of coconut milk

5 kaffir lime leaves

200g (1 cup) basmati rice

500ml (2 cups) water

finely sliced chillies, to
  garnish (optional)

Add the onion, garlic, ginger, coriander, the cardamom seeds, lemongrass, red chilli, tamarind paste, 2 tablespoons of the oil and the sugar to a blender and blitz until smooth.

Pour the remaining oil into a hot deep pan, add the beef and fry until brown, around 8 minutes. Add the paste, cinnamon stick and star anise and cook for a further minute, then add the coconut milk and kaffir leaves and allow to simmer for an hour at a medium–high heat (bubbling). This can be left and just stirred occasionally as the aim is to reduce the milk and be left with a dryish curry, so after an hour, decrease the heat and stir occasionally until the sauce has evaporated to a thick curry paste.

Add the rice with double the amount of water to a pan and bring to the boil. Once boiling, cook for 3 minutes, turn off the heat and put a lid on the pan so the rice can carry on steaming for 7–8 minutes. Do not stir as you want the rice to steam, absorb the water and fluff up.

Serve the curry spooned over the rice with a scattering of the sliced chillies, if desired.

SPATCHCOCK CHICKEN & CAVOLO NERO BAKE WITH ROAST GARLIC MASH

Cooking time: 1 hour 10 minutes
Difficulty: Hard

This one takes a little preparation with the roasted garlic, but once this is done you'll have the tastiest tray bake with the most incredible succulent chicken, crispy cavolo nero and buttery garlic mash.

1 small chicken

1½ tablespoons olive oil

1 garlic bulb

1 tablespoon tomato paste

8 basil leaves, finely chopped

4 large cavolo nero
   leaves, chopped

150g chestnut mushrooms,
   quartered

50g butter

2 large potatoes, peeled
   and roughly chopped

70ml milk

salt and pepper

Preheat the oven to 180°C/160°C fan/gas 4.

Turn the chicken breast-side down. Using a sharp knife, cut through the back bone to the inside, then press down to crack into a spread position. Place breast-side up in an oven tray, drizzle with 1 tablespoon of oil and roast for 30 minutes.

Cut the tip off the garlic bulb, just enough to see inside each clove, then peel back the outer skin, but not enough for the garlic to fall apart. Drizzle the remaining oil and sprinkle some salt into the cloves, wrap with foil leaving the top exposed and cook with the chicken (take out after 35 minutes).

Mix the tomato paste, basil and seasoning together to make a paste. Take the garlic, squeeze out all but three of the cloves and mix in. Take out the chicken and use a spoon to spread the mixture all over. Return to the oven for 20 minutes. Take out and add the cavolo nero, mushrooms and half the butter around the greens. Roast for another 15 minutes.

Meanwhile, cook the potatoes in a pan of salted boiling water for 15 minutes until soft. Drain, then add the remaining butter and milk. Mash until smooth with the remaining garlic. Add the mash to each plate and serve with the chicken, drizzled with stock from the pan, mushrooms and cavolo nero.

BASKET

3

RELAXED

IF YOU HAVE A BIT MORE TIME TO COOK
THIS WEEK, THEN THIS BASKET IS PERFECT.
THE HASSELBACK CHICKEN AND THE COD WITH
PESTO FETTUCCINE ARE BEAUTIFUL DISHES
FOR EASY ENTERTAINING, WHILE IT'S
WORTH MAKING EXTRA EFFORT OVER THE
STEAK-&-ALE HOT POT.

MENU FOR THE WEEK AHEAD

MONDAY

Sweet Potatoes Loaded with Chilli & Guacamole

TUESDAY

Hasselback Stuffed Chicken with
Rosemary Roast Wedges

WEDNESDAY

Tonkatsu Pork with Fluffy Rice & Miso
Shredded Cavolo Nero

THURSDAY

Pangrattato-Topped Cod
with Spinach Pesto Fettuccine

FRIDAY

Buttermilk Chicken & Chilli-Dusted Corn

SATURDAY

Crispy Tofu Pad Thai

SUNDAY

Steak-&-Ale Dauphinoise-Topped
Hot Pot with Buttered Greens

SHOPPING LIST FOR THE WEEK AHEAD

BASKET

MEAT & FISH

400g braising steak

2 chicken breasts

2 x 120g cod steaks

2 x 225g pork chops

DAIRY & EGGS

300ml double cream

4 eggs

2 tablespoons mascarpone

400ml milk

100g mozzarella

40g Parmesan cheese

2 tablespoons yogurt

VEGETABLES

100g baby spinach

300g bean sprouts

3 carrots

100g cavolo nero

250g chestnut
   mushrooms

2 corn cobs

8 garlic cloves

2 teaspoons crushed
   ginger

100g green cabbage

1.4kg Maris Piper potatoes

3 onions

3 red chillies

4 spring onions

2 sweet potatoes

160g watercress, spinach
   and rocket salad

HERBS

20g basil

16 sprigs of coriander

4 sprigs of parsley

3 sprigs of rosemary

9 sprigs of thyme

FRUIT

1 avocado

1 lemon

2 limes

GENERAL

500ml bottle of ale

½ crusty bread roll

400g tin of chopped
   tomatoes

200g fettuccine

200g flat rice noodles

1 tablespoon miso paste

100g panko breadcrumbs

10 peanuts

100g pine nuts

400g tin of red
   kidney beans

1 teaspoon sesame seeds

4 sun-dried tomatoes

1 tablespoon tamarind
   paste

150g firm tofu

200g bag of tortilla chips

CUPBOARD

basmati rice

bay leaves

beef stock

brown sugar

butter

chilli flakes

cumin powder

light spelt flour

mayonnaise

olive oil

salt and pepper

smoked paprika

soy sauce

sugar

tomato ketchup

tomato paste

vegetable oil

Worcestershire sauce

SWEET POTATOES LOADED WITH CHILLI & GUACAMOLE

Cooking time: 35 minutes
Difficulty: Easy

A vegetarian chilli with oven-baked sweet potatoes, finished with flavoursome guac and cooling yogurt. This is a great recipe for the start of the week.

2 sweet potatoes
1 tablespoon olive oil
1 onion, peeled and finely diced
2 teaspoons cumin powder
2 garlic cloves, peeled and crushed
2 teaspoons smoked paprika
6 sprigs of coriander,
    5 finely chopped
400g tin of chopped tomatoes
400g tin of red kidney beans
squeeze of lime juice
1 avocado, peeled and stoned
2 tablespoons yogurt
salt and pepper
finely sliced chillies, to
    garnish (optional)

Preheat the oven to 200°C/180°C fan/gas 6.

Bake the sweet potatoes for about 35 minutes until tender.

Meanwhile, add the oil and three-quarters of the onion to a pan over a medium heat and cook for around 5 minutes until starting to soften. Add the cumin, three-quarters of the garlic, the paprika, 2 sprigs of finely chopped coriander and some seasoning and cook for 1 minute. Add the tomatoes, kidney beans and a splash of water if too thick. Cook for 20 minutes at a simmering heat.

Add the remaining onion and finely chopped coriander, a squeeze of lime, the remaining garlic and the avocado to a bowl, season and mash together to form the guacamole.

Serve the sweet potatoes split open, loaded with chilli and topped with guac, yogurt, chilli slices and the remaining few coriander leaves.

HASSELBACK STUFFED CHICKEN WITH ROSEMARY ROAST WEDGES

Cooking time: 50 minutes
Difficulty: Hard

Hasselbacking the chicken is a great technique that gets the flavours all through the meat and helps the chicken to stay juicy throughout.

100g baby spinach

2 tablespoons mascarpone

4 sun-dried tomatoes,
    roughly chopped

2 chicken breasts

4 sprigs of thyme,
    roughly chopped

700g Maris Piper potatoes

1 tablespoon olive oil, plus
    extra to drizzle

2 sprigs of rosemary, chopped

100g mozzarella, grated

80g watercress, spinach
    and rocket salad

salt and pepper

Preheat the oven to 220°C/200°C fan/gas 7.

Wilt the spinach by adding it to boiling water for 10–15 seconds. Drain, then pat dry with paper towels. Mix the mascarpone with the spinach and sun-dried tomatoes.

Hasselback the chicken by cutting small lines from the top of each breast to about three-quarters through. Spread the spinach mixture from a spoon into the pre-cut gaps. Add the chicken to a baking tray, then sprinkle the thyme over the top.

Cut the potatoes into small chunky wedges and cook in salted boiling water for 5–6 minutes. Drain, season and add to a baking tray along with the oil and rosemary, tossing the potatoes so they are all evenly coated. Place the potatoes tray at the top of the oven for 30 minutes, tossing regularly. After 10 minutes, add the chicken on a shelf under the potatoes for the final 20 minutes. Swap the trays and scatter the mozzarella over the chicken. Cook for a further 7–8 minutes until the cheese is golden.

Serve the chicken with the rosemary potatoes and a side salad of watercress, rocket and spinach, drizzled with oil and seasoned with salt and pepper.

TONKATSU PORK WITH FLUFFY RICE & MISO SHREDDED CAVOLO NERO

Cooking time: 30 minutes
Difficulty: Moderate

Tender pork, flattened and panko'd to give it an ultra-crunchy crust, is perfect with this homemade tonkatsu sauce and simple sides of rice and greens.

---

2 x 225g pork chops, removed from the bone and trimmed of fat
200g (1 cup) basmati rice
500ml (2 cups) water
vegetable oil
1 egg, whisked
2 tablespoons light spelt flour
100g panko breadcrumbs
1 tablespoon tomato ketchup
1 tablespoon Worcestershire sauce
1 tablespoon soy sauce
1 garlic clove, peeled and crushed
1 teaspoon peeled and minced ginger
1 teaspoon sugar
100g cavolo nero, finely shredded
1 tablespoon miso paste
1 teaspoon sesame seeds
salt and pepper

Lay the pork steaks between two sheets of baking paper or cling film and flatten using a rolling pin. You want these to be nice and thin to cook quickly.

Add the rice with double the amount of water to a pan and bring to the boil. Once boiling, cook for 3 minutes, turn off the heat and put a lid on the pan so the rice can carry on steaming for 7–8 minutes. Do not stir as you want the rice to steam, absorb the water and fluff up.

Heat up 2cm oil in a frying pan to 180°C (350°F) – this usually takes about 8 minutes over a high heat. Add the egg to a dish, the flour and some seasoning to another and the breadcrumbs to a third. Take one steak and place both sides into the flour, then into the egg, then into the breadcrumbs. Lay it away from you into the oil and repeat with the second steak. Cook for 1–2 minutes per side until golden.

Add the ketchup, Worcestershire and soy sauces, garlic, ginger, sugar and a splash of water to a pan, bring to the boil and cook for 3–4 minutes until thick.

Cook the cavolo nero in a frying pan with a little oil until starting to crisp up. Add the miso, sesame seeds and a splash of water if you'd prefer it to be a bit more steamed. Serve the sliced pork on top of the rice with the cavolo nero. Drizzle over the tonkatsu sauce or serve in a bowl to the side.

PANGRATTATO-TOPPED COD WITH SPINACH PESTO FETTUCCINE

Cooking time: 30 minutes
Difficulty: Moderate

A delicious midweek meal with a crispy topping for the cod and homemade pesto for the fettuccine. The fish and pasta can both also be eaten as separate dishes or with different sides – experiment!

30g butter
40g Parmesan cheese, grated
½ crusty bread roll
2 sprigs of thyme, leaves only
2 garlic cloves, peeled
100g baby spinach
100g pine nuts
20g basil
75ml olive oil
2 x 120g cod steaks
200g fettuccine
salt and pepper

Preheat the oven to 180°C/160°C fan/gas 4.

Add the butter, Parmesan, bread, thyme, salt and pepper and one clove of garlic to a food processor and lightly blitz. Empty into a dish.

Now add the baby spinach, other garlic clove, the pine nuts, basil, seasoning and a dash of olive oil to the food processor and blitz until smooth.

Add the cod to a baking tray, season and bake for 8 minutes. After this time, sprinkle the pangrattato over the top of the steaks and put back in the oven for 3–4 minutes until the crumbs begin to brown.

Meanwhile, add your fettuccine to a pan of salted boiling water and cook until beginning to soften. Drain, reserving some of the pasta water.

Now take a frying pan and add a dash of oil. Add the fettuccine and pesto to the frying pan and cook for 2–3 minutes, adding a splash of the reserved pasta water to loosen the pasta.

Arrange the pasta in two bowls and lay the fish over the top. Serve with a swirl of olive oil and a little seasoning.

BUTTERMILK CHICKEN & CHILLI-DUSTED CORN

Cooking time: 30 minutes
Marinating time: 3 hours
Difficulty: Moderate

Chicken covered in crispy tortilla crumbs and cooked in the oven, for a healthier alternative to fried chicken. Serve with chilli-buttered corn and a simple salad.

400ml milk

juice and zest of 1 lemon

2 chicken breasts

1 teaspoon chilli flakes

1 teaspoon crushed and
   peeled ginger

½ garlic clove, peeled and crushed

1 teaspoon smoked paprika

200g bag of tortilla chips

2 teaspoons vegetable oil

2 teaspoons butter, softened

2 corn cobs

80g watercress, spinach
   and rocket salad

mayonnaise, to serve

grated zest of ½ lime, to serve

chilli powder, to serve

Preheat the oven to 180°C/160°C fan/gas 4.

Add the milk to a bowl or ziplock bag with the juice of the lemon. This will begin the curdling process to give you something very similar to buttermilk.

Slice the chicken breasts into four pieces (each breast into two), add to the milk and leave in the fridge to marinate for at least 3 hours.

Add three-quarters of the chilli flakes, the ginger, garlic, paprika and the zest of the lemon to a bowl, then add the tortillas to another bowl and crush until you have a breadcrumb-like dusting.

Once marinated, drain the chicken, then dust with the spice blend and add straight to the crushed crumbs. Lay out on a baking paper-lined baking tray and drizzle with the oil. Bake for 20 minutes.

Meanwhile, add the butter to the remaining chilli flakes and rub over the two corn cobs. These can go in the oven for the final 12–14 minutes, turning both the chicken and corn halfway through.

Serve everything on a large platter with the salad and a bowl of mayonnaise mixed with the lime zest and sprinkled with chilli powder.

CRISPY TOFU PAD THAI

Cooking time: 20 minutes
Difficulty: Easy

Surely everyone has their favourite pad Thai recipe? I created this one after spending many weeks exploring Thailand in my twenties. Such a simple dish, but so filling and flavoursome.

200g flat rice noodles

1 teaspoon brown sugar

2 tablespoons soy sauce

1 garlic clove, peeled and crushed

1 tablespoon tamarind paste

1 tablespoon vegetable oil

150g firm tofu, cubed and
  patted dry

½ onion, peeled and
  finely chopped

1 carrot, peeled and sliced into
  thin matchsticks

300g bean sprouts

1 small red chilli, finely sliced

4 spring onions, trimmed and cut
  in half and into thin slithers

3 eggs

10 sprigs of coriander,
  roughly chopped

1 lime

10 peanuts, crushed

Add the rice noodles to boiling water and cook for around 3–4 minutes until just about starting to soften. Rinse with cold water ready for adding later.

Add the brown sugar, soy sauce, garlic and tamarind paste to a bowl and mix thoroughly.

Pour the oil into a hot wok-type pan, add the tofu and onion and cook for about 2 minutes until starting to crisp and brown. Add the carrot and cook for a further minute, then add the noodles and bean sprouts and cook for 30 seconds. Mix in the sauce mixture along with the chilli and spring onions.

Move all the vegetables to the side of the pan and crack the eggs into the empty space. Move the egg mixture around quickly to make it scramble and after about 30 seconds, or when the egg is starting to firm up, quickly stir all the eggs through the noodle and veg mix. Lastly, add three-quarters of the coriander and mix in.

Sprinkle the rest of the coriander over the top along with a squeeze of lime and serve topped with the crushed peanuts.

STEAK-&-ALE DAUPHINOISE-TOPPED HOT POT WITH BUTTERED GREENS

Cooking time: 2 hours 20 minutes
Difficulty: Moderate

This is the perfect combination of two classics: my rich steak-and-ale casserole pimped up with a crusty dauphinoise topping. Lots for leftovers too.

400g braising steak, thinly sliced
1 tablespoon light spelt flour
1 tablespoon vegetable oil
250ml beef stock
1 onion, peeled and sliced
2 carrots, peeled and cut
    into cubes
250g chestnut mushrooms, sliced
2 tablespoons tomato paste
1½ teaspoons smoked paprika
1 teaspoon Worcestershire sauce
4 sprigs of parsley, finely chopped
1 sprig of rosemary,
    roughly chopped
3 sprigs of thyme
3 garlic cloves, peeled and crushed
2 bay leaves
500ml bottle of ale (I used
    bottled Guinness)
700g Maris Piper potatoes, peeled
300ml double cream
100g green cabbage, sliced
50g butter
salt and pepper

Preheat the oven to 180°C/160°C fan/gas 4.

Add the beef to a bowl, mix with the flour and season, making sure the beef is all coated equally. Pour the oil into a deep cooking pot, add the beef and cook until starting to brown and get charred on the outside, then transfer to another dish.

Add a dash of stock to the pan to deglaze the sticky beef flavouring, then add the onion, carrot and mushrooms and cook for 3 minutes until they start to colour nicely. Add the tomato paste, paprika, Worcestershire sauce, parsley, rosemary, thyme and 1 crushed garlic clove and cook for 1 minute. Now add the bay leaves, ale, beef and remaining stock and place a lid on. Bake in the oven for 1 hour, then take the lid off and cook for 30 minutes until the sauce thickens.

Transfer the beef mix to an ovenproof dish and slice the potatoes thinly into almost crisp-like slices. Layer the potatoes over the beef filling, going on top and down each side, adding a small amount of cream and the remaining garlic between the layers and repeating with two to three layers. Bake for a further 30 minutes at 200°C/180°C fan/gas 6.

Place the cabbage and butter into a lidded pan, season and steam for 4 minutes. Serve a scoop of hot pot with a side of the buttered cabbage.

BASKET

4

LIGHT

....

THIS BASKET IS GREAT FOR THOSE
WARMER EVENINGS WHEN YOU FANCY
A SLIGHTLY LIGHTER WEEK.

....

MENU FOR THE WEEK AHEAD

MONDAY
Sweet Potato Gnocchi with Popped
Tomatoes & Sage Parmesan Oil

TUESDAY
Middle-Eastern Lamb with Toasted Breads

WEDNESDAY
Spaghetti alla Norma

THURSDAY
Tomato Feta Salad with
Toasted Pistachio, Apple & Pomegranate

FRIDAY
Spicy Sesame Sea Bass Noodles

SATURDAY
Mexican Smoked Chicken Burger,
Avocado & Sweet Potato Crisps

SUNDAY
Bombay Chicken & Hasselback Potato Bake

SHOPPING LIST FOR THE WEEK AHEAD

BASKET

MEAT & FISH
2 chicken breasts
4 chicken thighs
400g lean minced
   lamb
2 x 90g sea bass fillets

DAIRY & EGGS
200g feta
500g Greek yogurt
50g Parmesan cheese

VEGETABLES
1 aubergine
175g baby corn
200g baby spinach
2 carrots
8 garlic cloves
1 teaspoon grated ginger
240g mixed leaves
   and beetroot salad
500g new potatoes
6 red chillies
2 red onions
3 large sweet potatoes
   (250g each)

HERBS
15 sprigs of coriander
3 sprigs of mint
3 sprigs of rosemary
1 sprig of sage
2 sprigs of thyme

FRUIT
1 apple
1 avocado
16 cherry tomatoes
1 lemon
1 pomegranate
9 large tomatoes

GENERAL
2 burger buns
2 teaspoons chipotle
   chilli flakes
275g fresh egg noodles
1 handful of pistachios
2 tablespoons sesame
   seeds
4 wraps

4 wooden skewers

CUPBOARD

brown sugar
butter
coriander seeds
cumin powder
curry powder
honey
light soy sauce
light spelt flour
olive oil
salt and pepper
spaghetti

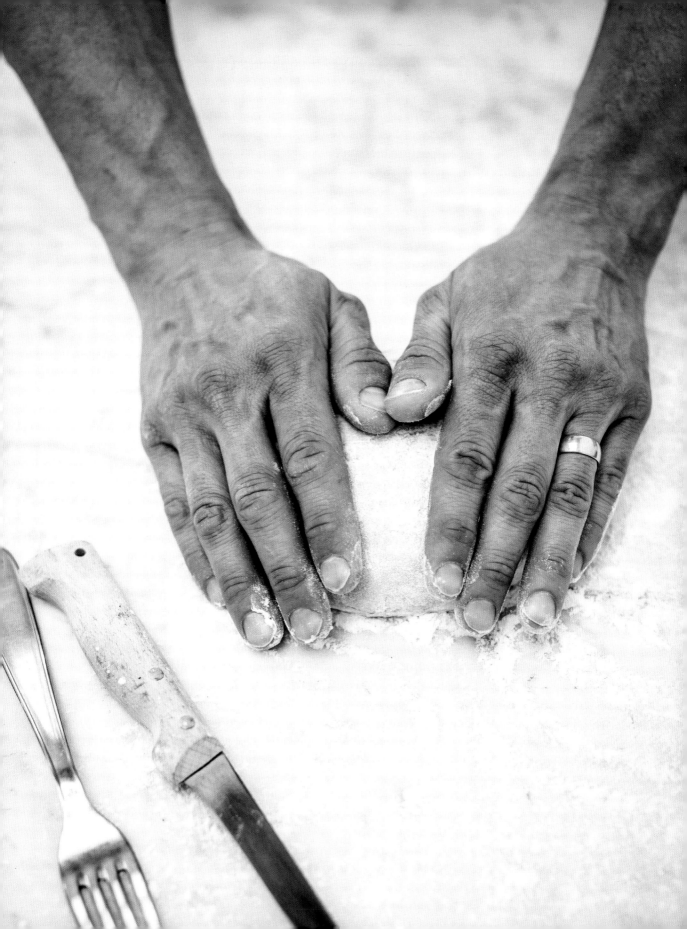

SWEET POTATO GNOCCHI WITH POPPED TOMATOES & SAGE PARMESAN OIL

Cooking time: 1 hour 15 minutes
Difficulty: Hard

This is the perfect filling, throw-together dish, which works so well with the fragrance of the herbs. It's a big portion meal, so if you have any leftovers, this one's great to take to work or use for an extra meal the next day.

2 large sweet potatoes (500g)
16 cherry tomatoes
270g light spelt flour,
    plus extra for dusting
25g butter
1 tablespoon olive oil
1 garlic clove, peeled and crushed
1 sprig of sage, leaves only
1 sprig of rosemary, chopped
25g Parmesan cheese, grated
salt and pepper

Preheat the oven to 200°C/180°C fan/gas 6.

Bake the potatoes for 45 minutes until tender. Remove and reduce the temperature to 180°C/ 160°C fan/gas 4. Add the tomatoes to an ovenproof pan with a pinch of salt and pepper and bake for 15 minutes.

Meanwhile, season the flesh of the sweet potatoes and add to the flour and 15g of the butter. Mash until it forms a soft consistency.

Dust a work surface with flour, cut the dough into three portions and gently roll the mixture into sausage shapes, rolling back and forwards until you have the same size along the line. Dust with flour so nothing sticks, then cut into 2–3cm sections, pressing along the back of each gnocchi with a fork. Fill a pan with salted water and bring to the boil. Add the gnocchi until it floats, then drain.

Pour the oil into a heated frying pan and add the garlic, sage and rosemary. Once warm, add the gnocchi and remaining butter. Allow the butter to bubble and move the gnocchi around to cook on all sides. Sprinkle with Parmesan and continue to move the gnocchi around the pan. Stir in the tomatoes, add more Parmesan and serve.

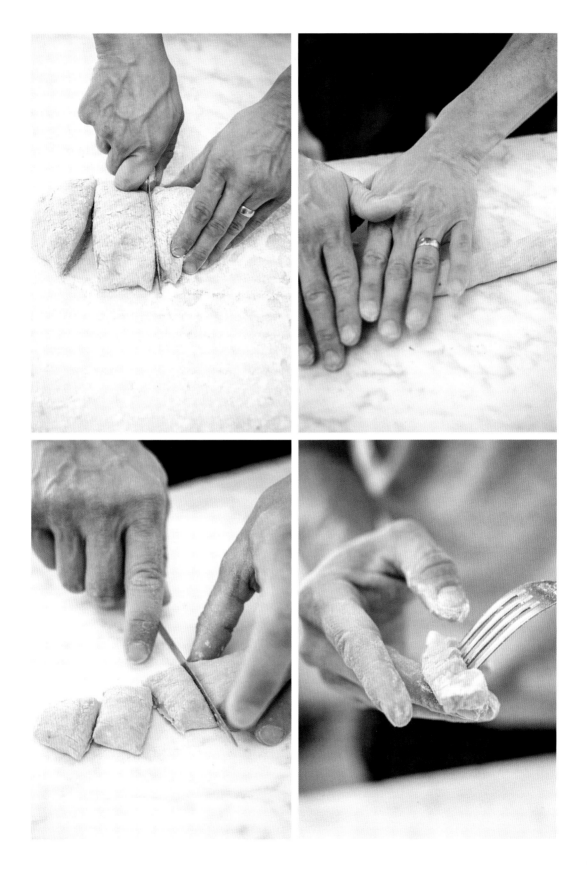

MIDDLE-EASTERN LAMB WITH TOASTED BREADS

Cooking time: 20 minutes
Difficulty: Easy

Fragrant and aromatic lamb skewers with the simplest flat breads, pomegranate and cooling yogurt, make this the perfect no-fuss evening meal.

400g lean minced lamb

2 teaspoons cumin powder

1 garlic clove, peeled and crushed

1 red chilli, finely chopped

1 sprig of rosemary, finely chopped

4 sprigs of coriander,
  finely chopped

4 wraps

80g mixed leaves and
  beetroot salad

1 sprig of mint, leaves only

100g Greek yogurt

juice of ½ lemon

seeds of ½ pomegranate

100g feta

¼ red onion, peeled and
  finely sliced

salt and pepper

4 wooden skewers, soaked in
  water for 30 minutes

Add the lamb, cumin, garlic and chilli to a bowl, then add the rosemary and coriander to the mix. Gently stir until well combined and season with a pinch of salt and pepper. Divide and shape into four even amounts and push onto the skewers in sausage-type shapes, forming the mixture around each skewer so that the skewer is central.

Heat a griddle pan and add the skewers, cooking evenly with char lines until the centre of each is cooked to your liking.

Take the wraps and toast in a frying pan until they puff up and create char marks. To serve, scatter the toasted wraps with the mixed leaves, mint leaves, a generous dollop of yogurt, a squeeze of lemon, the pomegranate seeds and crumbled feta. Finish with the red onion and lamb skewers, wrap up and enjoy!

SPAGHETTI ALLA NORMA

Cooking time: 45 minutes
Difficulty: Easy

Crispy aubergine is scattered over the most incredible tomato sauce in this classic spaghetti dish, here with a coriander twist. The secret to this recipe is definitely the sauce. It takes a little time, but once it's made it's so worth it.

2 garlic cloves, peeled and crushed
2 carrots, peeled and chopped
4 large tomatoes, chopped
1 red onion, peeled and chopped
4 tablespoons olive oil,
    plus an extra splash
1 teaspoon coriander seeds
1 sprig of rosemary, leaves only
250ml water
1 aubergine
200g spaghetti
juice of ½ lemon
25g Parmesan cheese, grated
3 sprigs of coriander, leaves only
salt and pepper

Add the garlic, carrot, tomato, onion, oil, coriander seeds and rosemary leaves to a deep saucepan with the water and a lid and cook over a low heat for 35 minutes until everything is soft.

Blitz in a food processor, season and set aside.

Meanwhile, finely chop the aubergine into small cubes, add a splash of olive oil to a pan and cook until brown on all sides, then set aside to dry.

Cook the spaghetti in a pan of salted boiling water until the desired texture, then drain and add to a frying pan along with the sauce. Squeeze in the lemon juice, heat thoroughly and serve with the aubergine scattered over the top, a sprinkle of Parmesan and a scattering of coriander leaves.

TOMATO FETA SALAD WITH TOASTED PISTACHIO, APPLE & POMEGRANATE

Cooking time: 15 minutes
Difficulty: Easy

When you want a lighter meal, this salad is perfect. Packed with beautifully paired ingredients, it makes the freshest of salads.

80g mixed leaves
  and beetroot salad
¼ red onion, peeled and
  finely sliced
seeds of ½ pomegranate
1 apple, cored and finely sliced
4 large tomatoes, chopped
1 tablespoon olive oil, plus
  an extra dash
1 handful of deshelled pistachios
100g feta
2 sprigs of mint
salt and pepper

Add the mixed leaves, red onion, pomegranate seeds, apple, tomato, olive oil and some salt and pepper to a bowl and mix together.

Add the pistachio nuts to a frying pan and heat with a dash of oil. Once hot, these are done.

Serve the salad on two plates, scattering with the nuts, crumbled feta and torn fresh mint.

SPICY SESAME SEA BASS NOODLES

Cooking time: 20 minutes
Difficulty: Easy

All the s's on this dish! Succulent soft fish with crispy skin and tasty sesame seed noodles, but with a little chilli punch for that extra zing.

2 sprigs of coriander, finely
   chopped, plus extra to
   garnish (optional)
½ red chilli, finely chopped
1 garlic clove, peeled and crushed
2 x 90g sea bass steaks
dash of olive oil
275g fresh egg noodles
2 tablespoons light soy sauce
1 teaspoon peeled and
   grated ginger
½ tablespoon brown sugar
2 tablespoons sesame seeds
100g baby spinach
finely sliced chillies, to
   garnish (optional)

Add the coriander and chilli to the garlic to make a fine paste. Score each fish on the skin side with three or four lines (this helps the fish to cook and not curl up). Add to a hot pan with a dash of oil and cook for 3–4 minutes max per side.

Add the noodles to a wok or frying pan with the soy sauce, coriander paste, ginger and sugar. Move the noodles quickly and add a splash of water if sticking, then add three-quarters of the sesame seeds along with the spinach. Cook until the noodles are hot and the sauce is all combined.

Add the noodles to two plates along with a piece of fish (skin-side up) and scatter with the rest of the sesame seeds, some coriander and chilli, if using.

MEXICAN SMOKED CHICKEN BURGER, AVOCADO & SWEET POTATO CRISPS

Cooking time: 30 minutes
Difficulty: Easy

Possibly the best chicken burger ever! This smoky and sweet burger is extra lean, packed full of flavour and ready in 30 minutes. The chipotle jam adds a little heat, while the cool avocado and yogurt perfectly balance everything out.

1 large sweet potato

1 tablespoon olive oil

2 garlic cloves, peeled and crushed

½ red chilli, chopped

2 sprigs of thyme, chopped

2 chicken breasts, chopped

2 teaspoons chipotle chilli flakes

500ml hot water

50g honey

2 burger buns

100g Greek yogurt

1 avocado, peeled, stoned
    and sliced

80g mixed leaves and
    beetroot salad

1 large tomato, sliced

salt and pepper

Preheat the oven to 180°C/160°C fan/gas 4.

Roughly slice the sweet potato into crisp-size bites and add to a baking tray. Drizzle with the oil and bake for around 15–20 minutes. Season with salt.

Add the garlic, chilli, thyme, chicken and salt and pepper to a food processor and blitz (this can also be done by finely cutting everything together).

Take out and shape into two burger-size patties.

Add the chilli flakes to a saucepan along with the hot water and honey. Simmer until you get a thick, jam-type consistency.

Add the burgers to a hot griddle pan and cook for 5 minutes each side or until the centres are piping hot. Toast the buns in a hot pan. To serve, spread a spoonful of yogurt over the bottom of each bun and add the avocado, burger and a generous scoop of the chilli jam. Finish with the mixed leaves and tomato and serve with the sweet potato crisps.

BOMBAY CHICKEN & HASSELBACK POTATO BAKE

Cooking time: 30 minutes
Difficulty: Moderate

The perfect one-tray bake: hardly any washing-up and all the goodness in just one tin. Tender spiced chicken with sweet-and-sticky hasselback potatoes, all finished with a drizzle of yogurt and spinach.

2 teaspoons curry powder

2 garlic cloves, peeled and crushed

3 red chillies, 2 chopped

200g Greek yogurt, plus
    extra to serve (optional)

4 sprigs of coriander, plus extra
    to garnish (optional)

2 teaspoons cumin powder

4 chicken thighs

½ red onion, peeled and chopped

500g new potatoes

2 teaspoons honey

1 tablespoon olive oil

175g baby corn

100g baby spinach

salt and pepper

Preheat the oven to 180°C/160°C fan/gas 4.

Add half the curry powder, the garlic, one whole chilli, the yogurt, coriander, cumin and salt and pepper to a blender and blitz.

Add the chicken to a roasting tray and pour over the yogurt mixture. Scatter the onion and half the chopped chilli amongst the chicken.

Cut the potatoes with little slices going three-quarters down each potato, but not all the way (I cut against a wooden spoon to help the cutting depth). Add to a bowl and mix with the honey, oil, remaining curry powder and some salt.

Add the potatoes to the chicken tray along with the corn and roast for 25–30 minutes. Serve with fresh washed spinach, an optional extra dollop of yogurt, some coriander and the remaining chilli.

BASKET

5

VEGGIE

LOTS OF VEGGIES IN THIS WEEK'S BASKET FOR A FULL VEGETARIAN WEEK. YOU DEFINITELY WON'T MISS THE MEAT IN THIS ONE AND, TRUST ME, THE BOLOGNESE IS AN ABSOLUTE GAME CHANGER!

MENU FOR THE WEEK AHEAD

....

MONDAY
Mushroom & Brandy Stroganoff

....

TUESDAY
Sweet Potato Channa Masala

....

WEDNESDAY
Aubergine Parmigiana

....

THURSDAY
Lentil & Mushroom Bolognese

....

FRIDAY
Spiced Peanut Noodles

....

SATURDAY
Fully Loaded Black Bean Quesadillas

....

SUNDAY
Cauliflower & Broccoli Cheese Pie

....

SHOPPING LIST FOR THE WEEK AHEAD

BASKET

DAIRY & EGGS
350g mature
   Cheddar cheese
300ml crème fraîche
1 egg
550ml milk
1 mozzarella ball
5 tablespoons grated
   Parmesan cheese
4½ tablespoons yogurt

VEGETABLES
3 aubergines
350g head of broccoli
2 carrots
350g cauliflower
1 celery stick
500g chestnut
   mushrooms
7 garlic cloves
1 teaspoon grated ginger
3 onions
1 large onion
1 red pepper
3 spring onions
200g sugar snap peas
2 sweet potatoes (about
   230g each)

HERBS
14 basil leaves
10 sprigs of coriander
4 sprigs of parsley
2 sprigs of rosemary

FRUIT
1 lime
2 tomatoes

GENERAL
400g tin of black beans
1 shot of brandy
1 bread roll
400g tin of chickpeas
4 tablespoons crunchy
   peanut butter
125g dried egg noodles
400g tin of green lentils
1.2kg passata
10 peanuts
1 sheet of puff pastry
200g tin of sweetcorn
4 wraps

CUPBOARD

basmati rice
butter
chilli flakes
coriander powder
cumin powder
dried oregano
garam masala
light spelt flour
olive oil
plain flour
salt and pepper
smoked paprika
soy sauce
spaghetti
vegetable stock

MUSHROOM & BRANDY STROGANOFF

Cooking time: 25 minutes
Difficulty: Moderate

This stroganoff packs a serious punch with the most luxurious mushroom and brandy sauce. Try your hand at flambéing this to really impress.

25g butter

1 large onion, peeled and
   finely sliced

250g chestnut mushrooms,
   finely sliced

1 garlic clove, peeled and crushed

2 teaspoons smoked paprika

1 shot of brandy

1 vegetable stock cube

150ml water

150ml crème fraîche, plus
   extra to serve

300g (1½ cups) basmati rice

750ml (3 cups) water

2 sprigs of parsley, chopped

salt and pepper

Add the butter to a preheated frying pan. Keep this on a high heat and add the onion and mushrooms and cook for 2–3 minutes until starting to soften. Add the garlic, smoked paprika and the shot of brandy – you can flambé at this point by tilting the pan away to an open flame or setting it alight with a lighter or match (be sure to keep the pan well away from you for safety reasons).

Simmer for a further 2–3 minutes until it starts to reduce, then season and tip in the crumbled stock cube with the water and crème fraîche. Stir the sauce, then leave to thicken over the heat.

Meanwhile, add the rice with double the amount of water to another pan and bring to the boil. Once boiling, cook for 3 minutes, turn off the heat and put a lid on the pan so the rice can carry on steaming for 7–8 minutes. Do not stir as you want the rice to steam, absorb the water and fluff up.

Once the stroganoff sauce has thickened, serve spooned over the fluffy rice with a dollop of crème fraîche and the parsley.

SWEET POTATO CHANNA MASALA

Cooking time: 30 minutes
Difficulty: Moderate

This is the perfect takeaway curry-in-a-hurry type dish, packed full of flavour and served with super-easy homemade chapatis. If there are any leftovers, this is great for lunch the next day.

1 teaspoon olive oil
1 onion, peeled and finely chopped
1 teaspoon garam masala
½ teaspoon chilli flakes
1½ teaspoons coriander powder
1 tablespoon cumin powder
1 garlic clove, peeled and crushed
1 teaspoon peeled and
  grated ginger
2 tomatoes, finely chopped
1 sweet potato, peeled and
  chopped into small cubes
400g tin of chickpeas, drained
500ml water
3 sprigs of coriander,
  roughly chopped
300g (1½ cups) basmati rice
750ml (3 cups) water
1½ tablespoons yogurt
salt and pepper

Chapatis
1 teaspoon vegetable oil,
  plus 1 tablespoon for cooking
125g plain flour
pinch of salt
80ml water

To make the chapatis, in a bowl add the oil to the flour and salt, then pour in the water a little at a time, mixing with a fork. Once it comes together, knead to form an elastic dough. If the mixture is too dry, add a splash more water, a little at a time, as some flours require more or less water to form a dough. Cover the bowl and leave for 15 minutes.

Add the olive oil to a frying pan and cook the onion until soft, then add the spices, garlic and ginger and cook for 1 minute. Add the tomatoes and cook for 3–4 minutes over medium heat until they break down. Add the sweet potato, chickpeas and water. Simmer until the sauce thickens and the sweet potato softens. Stir through most of the coriander.

Meanwhile, add the rice with double the amount of water to another pan and bring to the boil. Once boiling, cook for 3 minutes, turn off the heat and put a lid on the pan so the rice can carry on steaming for 7–8 minutes. Do not stir as you want the rice to steam, absorb the water and fluff up.

Knead the dough on a floured surface and cut into four balls, then roll out each to a small plate size. Add the oil to a hot pan and cook each chapati on both sides, forming small char-mark blisters. Coat with a little oil and cook again until they puff up.

Serve the curry over the rice with the chapatis, remaining coriander and a dollop of yogurt.

AUBERGINE PARMIGIANA

Cooking time: 45 minutes
Difficulty: Moderate

This easy version of the Italian classic of layered aubergine, tomato, mozzarella and Parmesan is a real weekday favourite. Serve with a simple tomato and cos lettuce salad dressed with olive oil, salt and pepper.

1 onion, peeled and finely chopped

1 teaspoon olive oil

3 aubergines, sliced into thin lengthways slices

700g passata

2 garlic cloves, peeled and thinly sliced

1 sprig of rosemary, finely chopped

10 basil leaves, finely chopped

3 tablespoons grated Parmesan cheese

1 mozzarella ball

½ bread roll, blitzed in a food processor

1 teaspoon dried oregano

salt and pepper

Preheat the oven to 180°C/160°C fan/gas 4.

Add the onion and oil to a frying pan and cook until soft, then remove from the pan and set aside. Cook the aubergine slices in batches in the hot frying pan until softened and brown.

Add 3 to 4 tablespoons of the passata to the bottom of a small oven dish. Scatter with a little garlic, a pinch of the rosemary and basil and add a layer of the aubergine along with a small layer of onion. Finally, season with a little salt and pepper and sprinkle with ½ tablespoon of the Parmesan.

Keep combining the same layers until you reach the top. For the top, use the last of the Parmesan, then tear up the mozzarella and scatter with the last of the rosemary, basil and garlic.

Scatter the breadcrumbs over the top along with the oregano. Bake for 20 minutes until golden.

LENTIL & MUSHROOM BOLOGNESE

Cooking time: 30 minutes
Difficulty: Easy

The key to this recipe is the really finely chopped mushrooms and the lentils – they give the bolognese its meaty texture. If you're extra hungry, serve this up with a little bit of garlic bread.

---

1 teaspoon olive oil

½ onion, peeled and finely sliced

1 carrot, peeled and cut into
   pea-size cubes

1 celery stick, cut into
   pea-size cubes

2 garlic cloves,
   peeled and crushed

250g chestnut mushrooms,
   finely chopped (or use a
   food processor)

400g tin of green lentils

4 basil leaves, finely sliced

500g passata

1 vegetable stock cube

200g spaghetti

2 sprigs of parsley, chopped

2 tablespoons grated
   Parmesan cheese

salt and pepper

Add the oil to a frying pan and cook the onion, carrot, celery and garlic over a medium heat for 5–6 minutes. Add the mushrooms and cook through until they darken, then add the lentils, increase the heat and cook for a further 2 minutes.

Add the basil to the pan along with the passata, crumbled stock cube and some salt and pepper. Simmer for 10–15 minutes until the sauce has reduced and thickened.

Meanwhile, cook the spaghetti in a saucepan of salted boiling water until soft to the pinch.

Drain the spaghetti and serve with the bolognese over the top, the parsley and grated Parmesan.

SPICED PEANUT NOODLES

Cooking time: 15 minutes
Difficulty: Easy

One of the simplest yet tastiest stir-fry dishes you can make and it'll be ready and on the table in minutes. You can use smooth or crunchy peanut butter – both will come out great – and any veg: just chop finely and throw it in.

125g dried egg noodles

splash of olive oil

1 teaspoon chilli flakes

1 carrot, peeled and sliced
  into matchsticks

200g sugar snap peas, halved

1 tablespoon soy sauce

4 tablespoons crunchy
  peanut butter

juice of ½ lime

2 sprigs of coriander,
  finely chopped

3 spring onions, trimmed and cut
  on the diagonal into small slices

10 peanuts, crushed

salt

Add the noodles to a pan of salted boiling water and cook until starting to soften, then drain.

Pour a splash of oil into a wok or high-sided pan. Add the chilli flakes, carrot and sugar snap peas and stir-fry for 1 minute. Add the soy sauce and peanut butter and cook, stirring the sauce through the veg, for around a minute.

Add the noodles and a squeeze of lime and mix together well, adding a splash of water if this is looking too sticky to loosen it, then stir in the spring onions and most of the coriander.

Serve the noodles with the crushed peanuts over the top and the remaining coriander.

FULLY LOADED BLACK BEAN QUESADILLAS

Cooking time: 25 minutes
Difficulty: Easy

These tasty vegetarian quesadillas are very easy to make and are loaded with spicy black beans, cheese, rice and a cooling yogurt.

1 teaspoon olive oil
½ onion, peeled and
    finely chopped
400g tin of black beans
½ teaspoon coriander powder
½ teaspoon cumin powder
5 sprigs of coriander,
    finely chopped
½ teaspoon chilli flakes
1 red pepper, deseeded
    and chopped
200g tin of sweetcorn
100g (½ cup) basmati rice
250ml (1 cup) water
4 wraps
50g mature Cheddar
    cheese, grated
juice of ½ lime
3 tablespoons yogurt

Add the oil to a pan and fry the onion for about 2–3 minutes, then add the black beans, spices, half the coriander, the chilli flakes, pepper and sweetcorn and cook for 2–3 minutes until the beans soften.

Meanwhile, add the rice with double the amount of water to another pan and bring to the boil. Once boiling, cook for 3 minutes, turn off the heat and put a lid on the pan so the rice can carry on steaming for 7–8 minutes. Do not stir as you want the rice to steam, absorb the water and fluff up.

To serve, add rice to one side of a wrap with spoonfuls of the bean and onion mixture over the top. Sprinkle with some of the cheese, remaining coriander, a squeeze of lime juice and 2 teaspoons of the yogurt. In a hot frying pan, fold over and lightly press to seal everything. Repeat with the remaining wraps and serve.

127

CAULIFLOWER & BROCCOLI CHEESE PIE

Cooking time: 30 minutes
Difficulty: Moderate

You'll love this twist on the classic Sunday roast side dish, turning it into a hearty weekend main, perfect for a chilly night.

---

1 cauliflower, cut into florets

1 head of broccoli, cut into florets

50g butter

5 tablespoons light spelt flour

550ml milk

150g mature Cheddar
  cheese, grated

4 tablespoons crème fraîche

1 garlic clove, peeled and crushed

½ bread roll

1 sprig of rosemary

1 sheet of puff pastry

1 egg, beaten

1 sweet potato, halved

salt

Preheat the oven to 190°C/170°C fan/gas 5.

Cook the cauliflower and broccoli in a pan of salted boiling water for 3–4 minutes, then leave to drain.

Bring a pan up to heat and add the butter. Melt and stir in the flour until it forms a paste that leaves the sides and base of the pan cleanly. Continue to cook for 1½– 2 minutes, then add the milk a little at a time, stirring regularly to form a smooth sauce. Once it starts to thicken, add half the cheese, the crème fraîche and garlic, stirring until melted.

Put the bread and rosemary into a blender and blitz until you get breadcrumbs. Add the cauliflower and broccoli to an oven dish and pour over the cheese sauce, knocking the dish to make sure it goes through the florets. Cover with the last of the cheese and the breadcrumbs.

Cut the pastry to the same size as the dish, brush with the beaten egg and put on a baking tray. Place the pie, baking tray, plus the sweet potato, into the oven and bake for 20–25 minutes until the pastry has puffed up, the crumbs and cheese are bubbling and crispy, and the potato is soft to the centre.

Pop the puff pastry on top of the cauliflower and broccoli and serve the pie with the squeezed open sweet potato halves.

BASKET

6

TWIST

YOU'LL FIND SOME OF MY FAVOURITE RECIPES IN THIS CHAPTER, WHICH I'VE GIVEN A LITTLE TWIST TO. THEY INCLUDE A CHILDHOOD DISH THAT MY WIFE AND I USED TO HAVE FROM OUR LOCAL VILLAGE CHIP SHOP – 'CODDLES'. FIND OUT MORE ON PAGE 147.

MENU FOR THE WEEK AHEAD

MONDAY
Lentil & Sweetcorn Dal with Rotis

TUESDAY
Smoky Pineapple Ribs with Hawaiian
Slaw & Butternut Wedges

WEDNESDAY
Fattoush Salad & Sesame Seared Tuna

THURSDAY
Sausage Bake with Balsamic Roasted
Onions, Butternut & Broccoli

FRIDAY
Beer-Battered Coddles, Chips & Minted Peas

SATURDAY
Maldivian Chicken Curry

SUNDAY
Rosemary-Crumbed Lamb Rack,
Sweet Potato Purée & Yorkshire Pud

SHOPPING LIST FOR THE WEEK AHEAD

BASKET

MEAT & FISH

2 chicken breasts
2 x 120g cod steaks
4-bone rack of lamb
8 pork ribs (4 per
    baby back)
6 sausages
2 x 120g tuna steaks

DAIRY & EGGS

4–5 eggs (250ml)
250ml milk
2 tablespoons yogurt

VEGETABLES

3 baby carrots
1 butternut squash
3 carrots
1 corn cob or 110g
    frozen sweetcorn
½ cucumber
16 garlic cloves
1cm piece of ginger
1 green chilli
3 onions, 1 small
200g frozen peas
1 handful of pea shoots
    or watercress
4 Maris Piper potatoes
½ red cabbage
1 red chilli
3 red onions, 1 small
1 large sweet potato (250g)
220g tenderstem broccoli

HERBS

11 sprigs of coriander
5 sprigs of mint
5 sprigs of rosemary

FRUIT

2 lemons
4 fresh pineapple rings
12 mixed tomatoes

GENERAL

2 crusty bread rolls,
    1 small
8 cardamom pods
400ml tin of coconut milk
11 curry leaves
4 tablespoons Guinness
    from a bottle
malt vinegar (optional)
150g moong
    dal yellow
175ml red wine
2 tablespoons
    sesame seeds
large pinch of sumac
2 tablespoons sweet
    chilli sauce

CUPBOARD

baking powder
balsamic vinegar
basmati rice
beef stock
butter
cinnamon sticks
cloves
cumin powder
cumin seeds
curry powder
Dijon mustard
honey
light spelt flour
olive oil
salt and pepper
smoked paprika
soy sauce
sugar
tomato paste
turmeric
vegetable oil

LENTIL & SWEETCORN DAL WITH ROTIS

Cooking time: 1 hour
Difficulty: Hard

Introducing sweetcorn to this dal really brings a fuller flavour to the dish and is something I learnt from a chef in the Maldives. Pair up with a doughy roti, perfect for dipping and scooping up the sauce.

1 litre cold water

½ teaspoon turmeric

3 garlic cloves, peeled and crushed

3 sprigs of coriander

150g moong dal
  yellow (washed)

75g butter

1 green chilli, finely sliced

1 small onion, peeled and
  thinly sliced

1 teaspoon cumin seeds

6 curry leaves

1 corn cob, kernels taken
  off using a sharp knife,
  or 110g frozen sweetcorn

1 teaspoon tomato paste

2 tomatoes, finely chopped

½ teaspoon sugar

juice of ½ lemon

140g light spelt flour

90ml hot water

50ml vegetable oil

salt and pepper

Add the cold water, turmeric, one crushed garlic clove, one roughly chopped sprig of coriander and the moong dal to a pan, bring to the boil and simmer for 35–40 minutes until softened. Depending on the texture, you can add a little more water at this stage if the sauce reduces too quickly and dries up. Season and, using a blender or a fork, mash the mixture. Set aside to cool.

Add 50g of the butter, the chilli, onion, remaining garlic, cumin and curry leaves to another pan and cook for 2 minutes, then add the sweetcorn and cook for a further minute. Add the tomato paste and cook for 1 minute, then add the tomatoes, sugar and a squeeze of lemon juice. Simmer for about 4 minutes until you have a thick mixture.

You can now add the moong dal mixture to the corn and combine both. If this looks too thick, add a dash of water, then simmer for a further 6 minutes over a medium heat.

Meanwhile, add the flour, hot water, ½ teaspoon salt and the oil to a bowl and mix together with a fork. Add more flour if it's too sticky, then roll into a ball and knead for 3–4 minutes until softened, stretchy and not sticky.

→

Sweetcorn Dal / continued

Flour the work surface and roll the bread dough into a circle. Heat the remaining butter and brush it over the bread dough, then roll up and cut the cylinder into four equal portions. Roll out each portion with flour until wafer thin, then add one at a time to a hot frying pan and allow to bubble for about 1 minute each side before turning over.

Serve the dal with the remaining chopped coriander over the top and use the rotis to scoop it up. You can serve the dal with rice as an alternative too.

SMOKY PINEAPPLE RIBS WITH HAWAIIAN SLAW & BUTTERNUT WEDGES

Cooking time: 40 minutes
Difficulty: Moderate

These are the most addictive thing I've ever made. The ribs are just incredible, especially paired with the fruity slaw. If you're not a fan of fruit with savoury, I'm hoping this one will change your mind.

1 teaspoon smoked paprika

6 garlic cloves, 1 peeled and crushed and the rest left whole and unpeeled

2 tablespoons honey

1 tablespoon soy sauce

2 tablespoons sweet chilli sauce

1 red chilli, finely chopped

4 fresh pineapple rings, 2 finely sliced or squashed, 2 chopped

8 pork ribs (4 per baby back)

½ butternut squash, deseeded and cut into chip wedges

1 sprig of rosemary, leaves only

1 tablespoon olive oil

¼ red cabbage

1 small red onion, peeled

3 sprigs of coriander, finely chopped

2 tablespoons yogurt

juice of ½ lemon

Preheat the oven to 180°C/160°C fan/gas 4.

Thoroughly mix the paprika, crushed garlic, honey, soy sauce, chilli sauce, half the chilli and the sliced pineapple in a bowl. Add the ribs to a baking tray (try and use a small one where the liquid will stay contained) and smother with the marinade.

To a second small baking tray, add the butternut wedges and the rest of the chilli, scatter with the rosemary leaves and the garlic cloves and drizzle with the oil.

Bake for 35 minutes, checking regularly and turning both the ribs and the squash. If the ribs need the liquid basted back over them, do so with a spoon.

Finely slice the cabbage and onion with a mandolin or sharp knife into slithers, then add to a bowl with the coriander, yogurt, a squeeze of lemon juice and the chopped pineapple. Stir until combined (the yogurt will start to go purple).

Serve the ribs with a side of crunchy butternut squash chips and a dollop of coleslaw.

FATTOUSH SALAD & SESAME SEARED TUNA

Cooking time: 5 minutes
Difficulty: Easy

This is an incredibly quick but impressive midweek meal of simple seared fresh tuna with the delicious Middle-Eastern bread salad – fattoush. The tuna is best cooked as rare as you dare!

2 tablespoons olive oil

large pinch of sumac

juice of ½ lemon

4 sprigs of coriander, leaves only

3 sprigs of mint, leaves only

3 baby carrots

6 mixed tomatoes, chopped

½ red onion, peeled and
    finely sliced

½ cucumber, sliced in half
    lengthways and then sliced

1 small crusty bread roll,
    broken into pieces

2 x 120g tuna steaks

2 tablespoons sesame seeds

vegetable oil, for frying

1 handful of pea shoots or
    watercress

salt and pepper

Add the olive oil, sumac, lemon juice, coriander and mint to a bowl, then season with salt and pepper. Chop the carrots straight down the middle and add to the mixing bowl along with the tomatoes, red onion, cucumber and bread and mix by swirling the bowl away from you.

Take the tuna steaks and press into the sesame seeds. To a piping hot pan add a small amount of oil and cook the tuna steaks for 30 seconds each side until medium-rare.

Serve the sliced tuna with the salad and dressed with pea shoots.

SAUSAGE BAKE WITH BALSAMIC ROASTED ONIONS, BUTTERNUT & BROCCOLI

Cooking time: 40 minutes
Difficulty: Easy

I love this dish, especially because you've got nearly everything in one pan – less washing-up and more time to enjoy! This recipe is also dairy free.

1 red onion, peeled and
    cut into quarters
½ butternut squash, deseeded
    and cut into long wedges from
    top to bottom
6 sausages
2 tablespoons olive oil
3 garlic cloves, peeled and
    roughly chopped
2 sprigs of rosemary,
    finely chopped
2 tablespoons balsamic vinegar
220g tenderstem broccoli

Preheat the oven to 200°C/180°C fan/gas 6.

Add the onion and squash to a small baking tin along with the sausages. Drizzle over the oil, scatter with the garlic and rosemary and make sure everything is mixed up together, then drizzle the balsamic vinegar over each segment of onion. Roast for 30 minutes, turning regularly.

Add the broccoli to a pan of boiling water and blanch for 3 minutes, then drain and add to the sausage tray bake. Cook for a further 6 minutes at 220°C/200°C fan/gas 7, then serve.

BEER-BATTERED CODDLES, CHIPS & MINTED PEAS

Cooking time: 30 minutes
Difficulty: Moderate

These little fish bites and their name comes from a small village I grew up in. The local fish-and-chip shop would do crazy things like deep-fried pizza, scraps and these amazing crunchy little fish bites. I had to keep the name going as I don't think I've ever seen a coddle since!

---

2 x 120g cod steaks, cut into
   long bite-size chunks
50g light spelt flour
4 tablespoons Guinness
   from a bottle
1 teaspoon baking powder
500ml vegetable oil
4 Maris Piper potatoes,
   peeled and cut into chips
200g frozen peas
2 sprigs of mint, leaves chopped
25g butter
½ lemon, cut into wedges
malt vinegar (optional)
salt and pepper

Pat dry the cod and leave on a paper towel. Take a shallow bowl, add a tablespoon of the flour and season. To another bowl, add the rest of the flour, the beer, baking powder and a pinch of salt and mix thoroughly, adding more beer if it's too thick.

Add the oil to a pan, making sure it is deep enough to take all the fish and not overflow the oil. Using a thermometer, heat the oil to 190°C (375°F).

Cook the chips in a pan of salted boiling water for 4 minutes. Drain, pat dry on paper towels and add to the hot oil for 3 minutes until starting to turn golden brown. Take out and allow to drain.

Now take the fish, dust with the seasoned flour and dip into the batter. Add to the oil, in batches so you don't overcrowd the pan, laying the fish away from you. Cook for 2–3 minutes, turning every minute, then drain. Once finished, add the chips back to the oil for 3 minutes until dark and crispy, then drain.

Cook the peas in a pan of boiling water for 1 minute, then drain. Add the mint and butter and mash with a fork or blender. Serve the peas with the fish, chips, and lemon wedges. Sprinkle with salt and vinegar.

MALDIVIAN CHICKEN CURRY

Cooking time: 1 hour
Difficulty: Moderate

After a winter break in the Maldives for New Year, I literally ate this curry seven times in one week for lunch or dinner. It's an absolute belter of a recipe and one I've adapted from a head chef on the island. Trust me on this one, this is next-level curry awesome!

1 tablespoon vegetable oil

4 cloves

8 cardamom pods

2 garlic cloves, peeled and crushed

5 curry leaves

1 cinnamon stick

2 onions, peeled and
    finely chopped

2 tablespoons tomato paste

1cm piece of ginger, peeled
    and finely chopped

350ml water

1 tablespoon curry powder

2 teaspoons turmeric

1 teaspoon cumin powder

4 tomatoes, finely diced

400ml tin of coconut milk

2 chicken breasts, cut into small
    bite-size pieces

200g (1 cup) basmati rice

500ml (2 cups) water

1 sprig of coriander, chopped

salt

Heat the oil in a pan over a medium-high heat and add the cloves, cardamom pods, garlic, curry leaves, cinnamon, a pinch of salt and the onion and cook for around 2 minutes, moving the ingredients around quickly in the pan. Add the tomato paste and cook for a further 30 seconds, then add the ginger, a splash of the water to stop it sticking, the curry powder, turmeric and cumin. Add the tomatoes and reduce down for 4–5 minutes.

Stir in the coconut milk plus the rest of the water and simmer over a high heat to start reducing the curry to a thicker, darker colour. This usually takes around 30 minutes. Add the chicken and simmer for a further 20 minutes.

Meanwhile, add the rice with double the amount of water to a pan and bring to the boil. Once boiling, cook for 3 minutes, turn off the heat and put a lid on the pan so the rice can carry on steaming for 7–8 minutes. Do not stir as you want the rice to steam, absorb the water and fluff up.

Remove the whole spices from the curry if you prefer, then serve the curry with the rice and a sprinkling of the coriander.

ROSEMARY-CRUMBED LAMB RACK, SWEET POTATO PURÉE & YORKSHIRE PUD

Cooking time: 1 hour
Difficulty: Hard

This is one of those recipes where everything comes together like a flavour marriage: herby lamb, crunchy yet soft Yorkies, silky smooth sweet potato and rich gravy– it's the perfect Sunday combo.

250ml (1 cup) milk

250ml (1 cup) eggs

100g (1 cup) light spelt flour

2 tablespoons vegetable oil

75g butter

2 garlic cloves, peeled and crushed

4-bone rack of lamb

2 sprigs of rosemary,
    finely chopped

2 teaspoons Dijon mustard

1 tablespoon olive oil

1 crusty bread roll, blitzed
    to crumbs in a blender

1 red onion, peeled and
    finely sliced

4 tablespoons balsamic vinegar

175ml red wine, plus a splash
    for the cabbage

500ml beef stock

¼ red cabbage, finely sliced

1 large sweet potato, peeled
    and cut into chunks

3 carrots, peeled and
    halved lengthways

salt and pepper

Preheat the oven to 220°C/200°C fan/gas 7.

Mix the milk, eggs, flour and a pinch of salt together, then add the oil to a large individual tin, cast-iron dish or muffin/Yorkshire tin and put in the oven. After 3 minutes, add the batter to the oil and cook for 25 minutes for the Yorkie to rise (you can always do this ahead of the main meal).

Meanwhile, add 25g of the butter and one crushed garlic clove to a hot pan. Season the lamb and cook on all sides for 7 minutes until nicely brown. You can add more butter and baste if you'd prefer a bit more caramelisation.

Mix ½ crushed garlic clove, three-quarters of the rosemary, the mustard and olive oil into the breadcrumbs. Place the lamb in a roasting tin, cover the rack with the breadcrumb mix and roast for 15 minutes.

Take the lamb out and set aside to rest, then add the remaining rosemary and garlic, the red onion and balsamic to the lamb juices and deglaze the tin for 2 minutes until the onion softens. Pour in most of the wine along with the stock and reduce the mixture until starting to thicken to a jus.

→

151

Lamb Rack / continued

Add the red cabbage to a separate pan along with a splash of red wine, a splash of water, salt, pepper and 30g of the butter. Cook for about 10 minutes until starting to soften.

Meanwhile, add the sweet potato and carrot to a separate pan of salted boiling water and cook until softened. Drain, then add the remaining butter to the sweet potato and carrot and mash to a purée (or use a blender). Season with salt and pepper.

Serve the lamb pink with the sweet potato purée, Yorkshire pudding, jus and red cabbage.

BASKET

7

SUMMER

THIS IS THE PERFECT SUMMER'S EVENING WEEK. A FRITTATA AND NIÇOISE SALAD MAKE USE OF THE BEST OF THE SEASON'S PRODUCE, WHILE A BEAUTIFUL PARMA HAM-COATED PORK FILLET AND PEACH STUFFING IS A SUMMER TAKE ON THE TRADITIONAL SUNDAY ROAST.

MENU FOR THE WEEK AHEAD

MONDAY
Pea, Feta & Mint Frittata with a
Lemon-Dressed Salad

TUESDAY
Griddled Tuna Steak, Niçoise Salad

WEDNESDAY
Feta & Chicken Meatballs in Lemon Spaghetti

THURSDAY
Thai Coconut King Prawn Curry

FRIDAY
Chorizo & Mushroom Toasts
with Sunny Side-Up Eggs

SATURDAY
Tear-&-Share Chicken Shashlik Naan

SUNDAY
Peach & Sage-Stuffed Pork Fillet with
Garlic Roasties

SHOPPING LIST FOR THE WEEK AHEAD

BASKET

MEAT & FISH
4 chicken breasts
190g chorizo
250g frozen/raw
   king prawns
80g Parma ham
600g pork fillet
   (in 1 piece)
2 x 120g tuna steaks

DAIRY & EGGS
8 eggs
200g feta
2 tablespoons milk
30g Parmesan cheese
300g yogurt

VEGETABLES
100g baby spinach
200g cavolo nero
800g Charlotte potatoes
300g chestnut mushrooms
½ cucumber
6 garlic cloves
2 teaspoons grated ginger
150g green beans
1 green pepper
1 small onion
100g frozen peas
2 red chillies
2 red onions, 1 small
1 red pepper
80g watercress, spinach
   and rocket salad
150g sugar snap peas

HERBS
30g basil
40g chives
20 sprigs of coriander
4 kaffir lime leaves
1 lemongrass stalk
30g mint
30g sage leaves

FRUIT
2 avocados
22 cherry tomatoes
3 lemons
1 lime
200g mango pieces
1 peach
2 large tomatoes

GENERAL
400ml tin of coconut milk
½ teaspoon ground cloves
100g black olives
2 slices of
   sourdough bread
2 slices of
   wholemeal bread

CUPBOARD

balsamic glaze
basmati rice
brown sugar
butter
chilli powder
cumin powder
fish sauce
garam masala
honey
olive oil
paprika
salt and pepper
self-raising flour
spaghetti
sugar
vegetable oil

PEA, FETA & MINT FRITTATA WITH A LEMON-DRESSED SALAD

Cooking time: 30 minutes
Difficulty: Easy

A simple weekday meal, perfect for using up any leftover veg in your fridge or for showcasing the best seasonal produce. Cook until golden brown, but still a little soft in the middle, and eat any leftover frittata cold the next day for lunch.

3 tablespoons olive oil

1 small red onion, peeled and
    finely sliced

200g Charlotte potatoes,
    thinly sliced

4 eggs

2 tablespoons milk

15g mint, roughly chopped

100g frozen peas

10g chives, finely chopped

120g feta

¼ cucumber

1 avocado, peeled and stoned

juice of ¼ lemon

6 cherry tomatoes, halved

80g watercress, spinach and
    rocket salad

salt and pepper

Preheat the oven to 170°C/150°C fan/gas 3.

Pour a tablespoon of the olive oil into a heated frying pan, then add the onion and potatoes and cook for 10 minutes until golden and soft.

Crack the eggs into a dish, season and add the milk. Add half the mint to the eggs along with the peas and half the chives. Crumble in the feta along with the cooked onion and potato and give it all a good mix. Grease a small round cake tin or small frying pan, add the mixture and bake for 20 minutes until cooked through and golden on top.

Meanwhile, using a potato peeler, ribbon the cucumber into small slithers. Thinly fan-slice the avocado.

For the dressing, in a bowl mix the remaining olive oil with the lemon juice, remaining mint and chives and some salt and pepper.

Mix the ribboned cucumber, avocado and cherry tomatoes together with the salad leaves and dressing. Serve the sliced frittata with the salad on the side.

GRIDDLED TUNA STEAK, NIÇOISE SALAD

Cooking time: 20 minutes
Difficulty: Easy

This recipe had to make it into the book as it's my wife's favourite! A hot niçoise salad is just a perfect healthy evening meal.

200g Charlotte potatoes

2 eggs

vegetable oil

2 x 120g tuna steaks

150g green beans

100g baby spinach

2 large tomatoes, chopped

100g black olives

½ red pepper, deseeded and
   thinly sliced

1 tablespoon olive oil

zest and juice of ¼ lemon

1 tablespoon balsamic glaze

salt and pepper

Cut the potatoes into halves and cook in salted boiling water for 6 minutes until they slide off an inserted knife. Take out and pat dry. Add the two eggs to the boiling water and cook for 5–6 minutes. Take out and add to cold water (iced if possible, otherwise they continue to cook).

Oil and season the tuna steaks and potatoes and add to a hot griddle pan, cooking the fish for 1 minute on each side for a nice rare centre. Take the tuna out to rest and then add the green beans to the potatoes and griddle for a further 2–3 minutes, until both the potatoes and beans have nice char lines.

Mix the spinach leaves, chopped tomatoes, olives and pepper with seasoned olive oil, a squeeze of lemon and a grating of the zest and spread out on two plates. Add the eggs, peeled and split in half, a scattering of the potatoes and beans, then top each portion with a sliced tuna steak. Swirl the balsamic glaze over to finish.

FETA & CHICKEN MEATBALLS IN LEMON SPAGHETTI

Cooking time: 30 minutes
Difficulty: Easy

These lighter meatballs use lean chicken and feta to create extra crust and flavour.

2 chicken breasts, chopped
1 garlic clove, peeled and crushed
15g basil leaves, finely chopped
20g chives
80g feta
½ slice of wholemeal bread
4 teaspoons olive oil, plus
   a splash for the spaghetti
200g spaghetti
juice of ¾ lemon
30g Parmesan cheese, grated
½ lemon, cut into wedges
salt and pepper

Add the chicken breasts, half the garlic, three-quarters of the basil, salt and pepper, chives, feta and bread to a blender and mix into a rough mince (don't overmix and add a dash of oil if sticking).

Take the mixture and roll into small balls around a ping-pong ball size. Add the oil and chicken meatballs to a heated frying pan and cook for about 10 minutes, turning regularly to get an even colour and cook all the way through. Remove and keep warm.

Meanwhile, add the spaghetti to a pan of boiling salted water and cook until al dente. Drain (reserving a little of the cooking water) and add to the frying pan over a high heat with a splash of oil and the lemon juice, the rest of the garlic and chopped basil. Add a splash of the reserved pasta water to loosen the sauce, then add half the grated Parmesan.

Serve the spaghetti with the meatballs, lemon wedges and a scattering of the remaining grated Parmesan.

THAI COCONUT KING PRAWN CURRY

Cooking time: 20 minutes
Difficulty: Easy

This is such a beautifully simple recipe and is ready in under half an hour. It is the perfect dish for using up any spare vegetables you have.

---

1 small onion, peeled

10 coriander leaves

zest and juice of 1 lime

¾ red chilli, finely sliced

4 kaffir lime leaves

1 teaspoon peeled and
grated ginger

1 garlic clove, peeled and crushed

1 teaspoon vegetable oil

400ml tin of coconut milk

2 teaspoons fish sauce

1 lemongrass stalk,
lightly smashed or cut
to release flavour

1 teaspoon brown sugar

200g (1 cup) basmati rice

500ml (2 cups) water

½ red pepper, deseeded
and thinly sliced

250g frozen/raw king prawns,
defrosted, cleaned and deveined

150g sugar snap peas, halved

Add the onion, three-quarters of the coriander, half the lime zest, the red chilli, two kaffir leaves, the ginger and garlic to a pestle and mortar and smash into a paste (or use a food processor).

Add the paste to a heated frying pan or wok with the oil and cook for 20–30 seconds, then add the coconut milk, fish sauce, the remaining lime zest and two kaffir leaves, the lemongrass and sugar and bring to the boil, stirring regularly.

Meanwhile, add the rice with double the amount of water to a pan and bring to the boil. Once boiling, cook for 3 minutes, turn off the heat and put a lid on the pan so the rice can carry on steaming for 7–8 minutes. Do not stir as you want the rice to steam, absorb the water and fluff up.

Add the pepper, king prawns and sugar snap peas to the hot coconut milk and cook for 2–3 minutes until the prawns turn pink.

Serve the rice and curry in separate bowls with a scattering of the remaining coriander and a final squeeze of lime.

CHORIZO & MUSHROOM TOASTS WITH SUNNY SIDE-UP EGGS

Cooking time: 15 minutes
Difficulty: Easy

This is great for breakfast, but even better for dinner. The smokiness of the chorizo and the runny eggs are just the perfect combination.

190g chorizo, finely sliced

150g chestnut mushrooms, cut into quarters

6 cherry tomatoes

2 teaspoons honey

10g chives, finely chopped

2 slices of sourdough, thick cut

1 teaspoon olive oil

2 eggs

1 avocado, peeled, stoned and thinly sliced

15g basil leaves, torn

2 teaspoons balsamic glaze

salt and pepper

Add the chorizo and mushrooms to a hot frying pan and cook for around 3 minutes until the chorizo releases oils to cook the mushrooms. Add the cherry tomatoes and cook until soft in the pan, then add a swirl of honey and half the chives. Transfer onto a plate to keep warm.

Using the oils from the pan, lightly toast the sourdough and add the remaining chives to the top of the bread.

Add a splash of oil to a small frying pan and crack in the eggs, cooking until the whites are firm, but the yolks are runny.

To serve, add the toast to two plates, top with the chorizo, tomato and mushroom mixture, sliced avocado, basil and sunny side-up eggs. Drizzle with the balsamic glaze and season with salt and a pinch of pepper.

TEAR-&-SHARE CHICKEN SHASHLIK NAAN

Cooking time: 30 minutes
Marinating time: 30 minutes
Difficulty: Moderate

This is the ultimate tear-and-share. Don't be scared to get messy – just rip off a piece of naan and wrap it up with all those amazing flavours.

300g yogurt

2 chicken breasts, cut into chunks

½ teaspoon paprika

2 garlic cloves, peeled and crushed

1 teaspoon cumin powder

½ teaspoon ground cloves

1 teaspoon garam masala

1 teaspoon chilli powder

juice of ¾ lemon

1 teaspoon peeled and
  grated ginger

10 coriander sprigs, ½ finely
  chopped, the rest left whole

1 red chilli, finely sliced into rings

15g mint leaves, chopped

200g (1 cup) basmati rice

500ml (2 cups) water

1 green pepper, deseeded
  and cut into cubes

1 red onion, peeled and cut into
  quarters and separated

130g self-raising flour

1 teaspoon sugar

200g mango pieces,
  finely chopped

salt and pepper

Mix 100g of yogurt with the chicken, paprika, garlic, cumin, cloves, garam masala, chilli powder, lemon juice, ginger, chopped coriander and chilli and marinate for 30 minutes. Mix the mint with 50g of the yogurt and a splash of water. Set aside.

Preheat the oven to 180°C/160°C fan/gas 4.

Add the rice with double the amount of water to a pan and bring to the boil. Once boiling, cook for 3 minutes, turn off the heat and put a lid on the pan so the rice can carry on steaming for 7–8 minutes. Do not stir as you want the rice to steam, absorb the water and fluff up.

Meanwhile, add the chicken, pepper and onion to a hot ovenproof griddle pan, turning after the chicken has released some fat to get char lines. Cook for 7 minutes, then transfer to the oven for 15 minutes.

Add the remaining 150g yogurt to the flour and sugar and mix well, season, roll into a ball, then flatten out into a large naan. Heat another griddle pan and char the bread until it puffs up, repeating on both sides until you get nice smoky char areas.

To serve, add the chicken mix, rice and mango to the naan with dollops of the mint sauce, sprinkling over the remaining torn coriander.

171

PEACH & SAGE-STUFFED PORK FILLET WITH GARLIC ROASTIES

Cooking time: 50 minutes
Difficulty: Hard

This is a proper Sunday roast with pork, roasties and veg, but it takes less than an hour in the oven and is perfect for two.

150g chestnut mushrooms,
   very finely chopped

50g butter

30g sage leaves

1 slice of wholemeal bread

1 peach, peeled, stoned
   and finely chopped

600g pork fillet (in 1 piece)

80g Parma ham

400g Charlotte potatoes

2 garlic cloves, peeled and crushed

splash of olive oil

10 cherry tomatoes

200g cavolo nero, chopped

salt and pepper

Preheat the oven to 220°C/200°C fan/gas 7.

Add the mushrooms and 10g of the butter to a hot pan and season, then add three-quarters of the sage and cook for 2–3 minutes.

Roughly chop the bread into crumbs and scatter into the mushrooms with the peach. Cook for a further 2 minutes until soft and brown.

Cut the pork fillet down the middle horizontally to create a pocket for the stuffing, then add the mushroom stuffing and tightly close together. Lay out a sheet of foil about twice the size of the fillet and cover the foil with layers of the Parma ham, creating a wrap effect ready to cover the fillet. Lay the fillet on the ham and tightly pull the ham over the fillet, then use the foil to tightly wrap the pork into a Christmas cracker-type cylinder. Twist both the ends of the foil and place into a heatproof tin.

Add the potatoes to a pan of salted boiling water and cook until starting to soften, drain and place in the same baking tin as the wrapped pork. Add the garlic, remaining sage and a splash of oil to the potatoes, season well and bake for 30 minutes, turning the potatoes every 15 minutes.

→

Pork Fillet / continued

Take the pork out of the oven and unwrap, adding the roast potatoes back to the oven whilst you do this (do not lose the juices created from the pork!). Add the fillet to a hot frying pan and cook along with the cherry tomatoes until the ham is crispy and dark and the tomatoes start to pop. Leave the fillet to one side to rest on a warm plate.

Add the cavolo nero to a separate pan with the remaining butter, season and cook over a high heat. If it starts to smoke, add a few splashes of water to start steaming it. This takes about 4–5 minutes.

Add the pork juices to a small pan and reduce them, then serve the fillet cut diagonally into circles and drizzled with any juices, along with the cabbage, tomatoes and crispy roast potatoes.

BASKET

8

SPICY

THIS WEEK HAS A NICE MIX OF SPICY DISHES AND A SUNDAY SHOW-STOPPER. GET THIS DISH RIGHT AND I PROMISE YOUR GIANT TOAD-IN-THE-HOLE WILL BECOME A WEEKLY STAPLE. FOR AN INTERESTING PRESENTATION, TRY LOADING THE VEG AND CHEAT'S GRAVY INTO THE YORKIE WHEN YOU SERVE IT UP.

MENU FOR THE WEEK AHEAD

MONDAY
Thai Tofu Green Curry

TUESDAY
Curried Chicken & Lime Kebabs

WEDNESDAY
Tastiest Cod & Veg One-Tray Bake

THURSDAY
Spicy King Prawn Linguine

FRIDAY
Vietnamese Pork Meatballs with Rice Noodles

SATURDAY
Chicken Saag

SUNDAY
Giant Toad-in-the-Hole

SHOPPING LIST FOR THE WEEK AHEAD

BASKET

MEAT & FISH

4 chicken breasts
2 x 120g cod fillets
300g frozen/raw
   king prawns
8 good-quality sausages

DAIRY & EGGS

2 eggs
300ml milk
8 tablespoons yogurt

VEGETABLES

400g baby spinach
1 carrot
½ cucumber
6 garlic cloves
200g fine green beans
100g kale
1 onion
1 pack of 3 mixed peppers
2 red chillies
7 spring onions
4 sweet potatoes,
   2 large (about 250g)

HERBS

6 basil leaves
7 sprigs of coriander
3 sprigs of rosemary
2 sprigs of thyme

FRUIT

30 cherry tomatoes
2 lemons
3 limes

GENERAL

400ml tin of coconut milk
180g linguine
crushed peanuts
   (optional)
125ml red wine
300g precooked
   rice noodles
3 tablespoons Thai
   green curry paste
200g tofu
2 wraps

4 wooden skewers

CUPBOARD

basmati rice
beef stock pots
butter
chicken stock
chilli powder
coriander powder
curry powder
garam masala
gravy granules
ground ginger
honey
light spelt flour
olive oil
paprika
salt and pepper
soy sauce
sunflower oil
turmeric
vegetable oil
white wine vinegar

THAI TOFU GREEN CURRY

Cooking time: 25 minutes
Difficulty: Easy

Light, spicy and ready in 25 minutes, this is the easiest and tastiest Thai curry you'll ever make. The recipe works as a great dinner and any leftovers can be taken to work the next day for a quick heat up for lunch.

400ml tin of coconut milk
2 tablespoons Thai green
   curry paste
300g (1½ cups) basmati rice
750ml (3 cups) water
2 tablespoons vegetable oil
200g tofu, cut into cubes
200g fine green beans
2 sprigs of coriander, chopped
salt and pepper
crushed peanuts, to garnish
   (optional)

Add the coconut milk and curry paste to a pan and heat until slowly bubbling.

Meanwhile, add the rice with double the amount of water to a pan and bring to the boil. Once boiling, cook for 3 minutes, turn off the heat and put a lid on the pan so the rice can carry on steaming for 7–8 minutes. Do not stir as you want the rice to steam, absorb the water and fluff up.

Pour the oil into a frying pan and cook the tofu until starting to brown. Season and add to the curry sauce.

Add the green beans to the curry and cook for a further 2 minutes.

Serve the rice in bowls with the green curry. Sprinkle with the coriander and garnish with the crushed peanuts, if using.

CURRIED CHICKEN & LIME KEBABS

Cooking time: 20 minutes
Marinating time: 1 hour
Difficulty: Moderate

Better than any kebab takeaway, these spicy kebabs are the perfect healthy alternative with yogurt raita and juicy chicken – all wrapped up with coriander, chilli and rice. It's the Middle-Eastern burrito!

---

1 tablespoon olive oil

½ teaspoon paprika

1 teaspoon honey

3 tablespoons yogurt

½ teaspoon curry powder

½ teaspoon coriander powder

1 garlic clove, peeled and minced

juice of 1 lime, plus lime
   wedges to serve

2 chicken breasts, cut
   into cubes

¼ cucumber

200g (1 cup) basmati rice

500ml (2 cups) water

2 wraps

1 red chilli, finely sliced

1 sprig of coriander, leaves only

salt and pepper

4 small wooden skewers,
   soaked in water for 30 minutes

Add the oil, paprika, honey, 1 tablespoon of the yogurt, the curry and coriander powders, garlic, half the lime juice and seasoning to a bowl. Add the chicken, mix thoroughly and marinate in the fridge, ideally overnight or for a minimum of 1 hour.

Meanwhile, add the remaining yogurt to a bowl and mix in the other half of the lime juice. Using a potato peeler, ribbon the cucumber into small slithers and add to the yogurt.

Add the rice with double the amount of water to a pan and bring to the boil. Once boiling, cook for 3 minutes, turn off the heat and put a lid on the pan so the rice can carry on steaming for 7–8 minutes. Do not stir as you want the rice to steam, absorb the water and fluff up.

Add the chicken to the skewers, threading it down into kebabs. Heat a griddle pan to high, add the skewers and cook for 6–7 minutes each side until the chicken has char lines and starts to caramelise. Test the centre to make sure it's cooked and piping hot all the way through. Remove to a plate to serve.

Add a wrap to the pan and warm both sides. Place half the rice in the centre, slide the chicken off two skewers onto the rice, drizzle with raita and scatter with a little chilli, coriander and a squeeze of lime. Repeat with the other wrap, roll up and enjoy!

185

TASTIEST COD & VEG ONE-TRAY BAKE

Cooking time: 25 minutes
Difficulty: Easy

This is the perfect 'get home from work and chuck it all in a pan' dish. Soft, flaky cod, vegetables bursting with flavour and all cooked within 25 minutes, not to mention hardly any washing-up! So, sit back, relax and let the one-tray bake do all the work.

---

2 large sweet potatoes,
   peeled and cut into wedges
2 peppers (different colours),
   deseeded and cut into wedges
10 cherry tomatoes
2 sprigs of thyme
1 tablespoon olive oil
1 tablespoon honey
4 spring onions, trimmed
2 x 120g cod fillets
1 lemon
100g baby spinach
salt and pepper

Preheat the oven to 170°C/150°C fan/gas 3.

Scatter the sweet potato and pepper wedges around a roasting tray. Add the tomatoes, thyme, salt, pepper, oil and honey and shake the tray to get everything coated. Chop the ends off the spring onions and add them whole. Place the fish, skin-side up, onto the vegetables. Cut the lemon in half, drizzle the juice over the fish and then add the lemon to the tray to allow it to roast and infuse the flavours. Roast for 22 minutes.

Once the time has passed, take the cod out of the pan and add the spinach, mixing it in with the veg. The delicious sauce you've created will cook the spinach whilst adding further flavour.

Serve the vegetables with the cod on top, drizzling any surrounding juices over the fish.

SPICY KING PRAWN LINGUINE

Cooking time: 15 minutes
Difficulty: Easy

This has to be my perfect 'go-to' recipe – it's so quick and simple, but packs in all the flavours and looks great served. Perfect for lunch or dinner, this pasta recipe goes from fridge to plate in less than 15 minutes.

180g linguine

1 teaspoon olive oil, plus
    more to drizzle

10 cherry tomatoes

½ small red chilli, sliced

2 garlic cloves, peeled and
    thinly sliced

300g frozen/raw king prawns,
    defrosted, cleaned and deveined

splash of white wine vinegar

100g baby spinach

6 basil leaves

1 spring onion, trimmed and
    thinly sliced

juice of ½ lemon

salt and pepper

Add the linguine to a pan of salted boiling water and cook for 10–12 minutes. Drain, reserving a little of the cooking water.

Meanwhile, pour the olive oil into another pan and cook the cherry tomatoes, chilli and garlic for 1 minute. Next, add the king prawns, a splash of white wine vinegar and season with salt and pepper, then add the linguine from the pan and a splash of the pasta cooking water, tossing the pan to allow everything to mix together. Cook for a further 2–3 minutes until the prawns are cooked. Finally, add the spinach, basil and the sliced spring onion. Swirl the pan again to combine everything.

Squeeze in the lemon juice and serve with a drizzle of olive oil and a grinding of pepper over the top.

VIETNAMESE PORK MEATBALLS WITH RICE NOODLES

Cooking time: 25 minutes
Difficulty: Easy

Succulent and spicy meatballs, veg and rice noodles, topped with crunchy peanuts and all served with the freshness of cucumber and fragrant coriander. This is another great lunchtime or evening meal choice, which can be enjoyed hot or cold.

---

1 sweet potato
½ red chilli, finely chopped
4 good-quality sausages
2 spring onions, trimmed and
  thinly sliced
1 garlic clove, peeled and crushed
1 tablespoon Thai green
  curry paste
juice of 1 lime
1 teaspoon honey
2 sprigs of coriander,
  finely chopped
light spelt flour, for the meatballs
vegetable oil, for frying
1 carrot, peeled and
  finely sliced into slithers
1 pepper, deseeded and finely
  sliced into slithers
300g precooked rice noodles
1 teaspoon soy sauce
crushed peanuts (optional)
¼ cucumber, sliced
  into matchsticks
salt and pepper

Add the sweet potato to a pan of boiling water and cook until soft, or microwave on full power for 8 minutes. Add the flesh of the sweet potato to a second bowl, spread it out to speed up the cooling process and add salt, pepper and the chilli.

Slice the sausages down their side and push out the meat from the skin into a bowl. Mix in the spring onion and garlic along with the curry paste, half the lime juice, the honey and half the coriander.

Once the sweet potato is cool, mix together the two bowls of ingredients. Shape into small meatballs and add a scattering of flour if needed.

Add a little oil and the meatballs to a hot pan and sear the outsides. Once brown on all sides, add a small amount of water to stop the meatballs from burning and steam the meat rather than caramelising too much. After 5–6 minutes, add the carrot and pepper, making sure you keep the pan moving to stop the ingredients sticking.

Next, add the noodles and soy sauce, cook for a further minute, then serve topped with the crushed peanuts, slithers of cucumber, a sprinkling of the remaining coriander and a squeeze of lime juice.

CHICKEN SAAG

Cooking time: 25 minutes
Difficulty: Easy

If you want a curry in a hurry, this is the dish for you. Quicker than ordering a delivery and definitely tastier. Light and spicy, this chicken curry is loaded with spinach and lower in calories than your average curry as it uses yogurt rather than cream for the sauce.

knob of butter or dash of olive oil

1 onion, peeled and finely chopped

2 chicken breasts, cut into cubes

10 cherry tomatoes

2 garlic cloves, peeled and crushed

2 teaspoons garam masala

1 teaspoon coriander powder

1 teaspoon turmeric

1 teaspoon chilli powder

1 teaspoon ground ginger

1 chicken stock cube

200ml water

300g (1½ cups) basmati rice

750ml (3 cups) water (for
   the rice)

5 tablespoons yogurt

2 sprigs of coriander,
   roughly chopped

200g baby spinach

salt and pepper

Put the butter or oil into a deep frying pan over a medium heat. Add the onion, allowing it to sweat down until soft and golden, then add the chicken, tomatoes, garlic and all the spices and cook until the tomatoes pop. Next, add the crumbled stock cube and 200ml water and leave to simmer for 10–12 minutes until the sauce reduces. Meanwhile, prepare the rice.

Add the rice with double the amount of water to another pan and bring to the boil. Once boiling, cook for 3 minutes, turn off the heat and put a lid on the pan so the rice can carry on steaming for 7–8 minutes. Do not stir as you want the rice to steam, absorb the water and fluff up.

Add 3 tablespoons of the yogurt and half the coriander to the curry and finally add the spinach and some salt and pepper and cook for 1–2 minutes until it wilts.

Add the rice to a dish and spoon over the curry along with a spoonful of the remaining yogurt and a sprinkling of coriander.

193

GIANT TOAD-IN-THE-HOLE

Cooking time: 45 minutes
Difficulty: Moderate

This is an English classic! The huge Yorkie will always rise and creates a centrepiece for the dish, served with beautiful kale, sweet potato mash and doused in ladles of my special 'cheat's gravy'. It's the ultimate hearty dish.

100g light spelt flour

300ml milk

2 eggs

4 good-quality sausages

1 large sweet potato,
   cut in half

3 tablespoons sunflower oil

3 sprigs of rosemary,
   2 cut up

100g kale

500ml cold water

1 teaspoon honey

2 tablespoons gravy granules

200ml hot water

1 beef stock pot

125ml red wine

knob of butter

salt and pepper

1 ice cube

2 mini loaf tins

Preheat the oven to 180°C/160°C fan/gas 4.

Add the flour, milk and eggs to a bowl, mix until smooth, drop in the ice cube and put in the fridge.

Add the sausages and the sweet potato to a baking tin and bake for 15 minutes to brown the sausages.

Pour the oil into the loaf tins and heat in the oven for 6–8 minutes. This must be really hot and should sizzle if you drag a rosemary sprig over. Add the sausages to the tins with the cut up rosemary. Pour the batter over the top of both. Place back in the oven for 20 minutes, by which time they should have risen and doubled in size.

Rinse and add the kale to a large lidded pan with the cold water, honey and seasoning. Place over a high heat on the hob and steam for 3–4 minutes.

Make a regular gravy mix with the granules and hot water. Bring to the boil and add the rosemary sprig, stock pot and wine. Let this simmer and you've got the best cheat's gravy you'll ever taste!

Squeeze the sweet potato out of its skin equally onto each plate and add the butter. Drain the kale and place next to the potato. Finally, add the toad-in-the-hole and drizzle around with the gravy.

BASKET
9

VARIETY

I WROTE THE RECIPES FOR THIS WEEK
WITH VARIETY IN MIND. MIDDLE EASTERN,
KOREAN, JAPANESE, FRENCH, ITALIAN
AND A NEXT-LEVEL TUNA JACKET POTATO!
TRUST ME, YOU'LL NEVER WANT
A TINNED TUNA JACKET AGAIN!

MENU FOR THE WEEK AHEAD

MONDAY
Falafel & Beetroot
Hummus Salad Pittas

TUESDAY
Chicken Katsu with Pickles & Spinach

WEDNESDAY
Ultimate Tuna Jackets

THURSDAY
Chicken Shawarma & Homemade Wraps
with Lemon Yogurt

FRIDAY
Beef Bulgogi with Rice & Spring Onions

SATURDAY
Spaghetti alla Puttanesca

SUNDAY
Beef Bourguignon Pithivier with
Thyme Mash & Shredded Greens

SHOPPING LIST FOR THE WEEK AHEAD

BASKET

MEAT & FISH

2 bacon rashers
5 chicken breasts
400g rump steak
400g sirloin or rump steak
2 x 150g tuna steaks

DAIRY & EGGS

2 eggs
30g Parmesan cheese
300ml yogurt

VEGETABLES

200g baby spinach
200g cooked beetroot
2 carrots
200g cavolo nero
250g chestnut
    mushrooms
1 cos lettuce
1 cucumber
10 garlic cloves
1cm piece of ginger
4 onions
2 jacket potatoes
2 Maris Piper potatoes
4 radishes
½ red cabbage
2 red chillies
4 spring onions

HERBS

30g basil
8 sprigs of coriander
3 sprigs of parsley
4 sprigs of thyme

FRUIT

2 apples
1 avocado
3 lemons
2 pears, 1 optional
8 tomatoes

GENERAL

4 tinned anchovies
14 black olives
1 tablespoon capers
2 x 400g tins of chickpeas
400g tin of chopped
    tomatoes
100g panko breadcrumbs
40g pine nuts
500g ready-to-roll
    puff pastry
175ml red wine
2 tablespoons tahini
2 wholemeal pitta breads

4 wooden skewers

CUPBOARD

basmati rice
beef stock
brown sugar
butter
cayenne pepper
chicken stock
cumin powder
curry powder
honey
light spelt flour
mayonnaise
olive oil
salt and pepper
sesame oil
smoked paprika
soy sauce
spaghetti
sugar
tomato paste
turmeric
vegetable oil
white wine vinegar

FALAFEL & BEETROOT HUMMUS SALAD PITTAS

Cooking time: 40 minutes
Difficulty: Moderate

Okay, so falafel isn't my favourite dish, but it is my wife's so it had to make it into the book. It also had to be a tasty version and have lots going on, which this one has with all the different flavour and texture combinations.

Hummus

200g cooked beetroot, drained
1 garlic clove, crushed
400g tin of chickpeas
2 tablespoons tahini
juice of ½ lemon
1 teaspoon cumin powder
90ml olive oil
salt and pepper

Falafel

2 tablespoons olive oil
1½ teaspoons cumin powder
1 garlic clove, crushed
1 onion, peeled and finely chopped
400g tin of chickpeas
1 egg, beaten
2 tablespoons light spelt flour
3 sprigs of coriander
grated zest and juice of ½ lemon

Salad

½ cucumber
2 wholemeal pitta breads
100g baby spinach
½ cos lettuce, torn into leaves
4 tomatoes, sliced
2 tablespoons yogurt

Preheat the oven to 200°C/180°C fan/gas 6.

Add the beetroot and all the hummus ingredients to a blender with a pinch of salt and pepper and blitz until smooth. Transfer to a bowl.

For the falafel, add 1 tablespoon of the oil to a heated pan with the cumin, garlic and onion and cook for 10 minutes until golden and soft. Transfer this to a blender, add a pinch of salt and pepper, the chickpeas, egg, flour, coriander, lemon zest and juice and the remaining tablespoon of oil and blitz until smooth. Roll into small golf ball-size amounts and place on an oven tray. Bake for 25–30 minutes, turning every 10 minutes. If they look dry or not browning, simple spray with a little extra olive oil.

Using a potato peeler, ribbon eight slithers from the cucumber.

To serve, heat your pitta breads in the toaster or oven and fill with the falafels, a dollop of hummus, the spinach, lettuce leaves, tomato, cucumber and a tablespoon of yogurt.

CHICKEN KATSU WITH PICKLES & SPINACH

Cooking time: 45 minutes
Difficulty: Moderate

While I know deep-frying can taste great with chicken, and katsu is usually exactly that, I've tweaked this oven version to taste just as good!

¼ cucumber

100ml white wine vinegar

1 teaspoon salt

1 tablespoon sugar

4 radishes, thinly sliced

2 tablespoons olive oil

1 onion, peeled and finely chopped

1cm piece of ginger,
    peeled and finely chopped

2 garlic cloves, crushed

1 carrot, peeled and chopped

1 apple, peeled, cored
    and chopped

3 tablespoons light spelt flour

1 teaspoon turmeric

2 tablespoons curry powder

2 coriander sprigs,
    finely chopped

1 tablespoon tomato paste

1 tablespoon honey

500ml chicken stock

100g panko breadcrumbs

1 egg

2 chicken breasts, butterflied
    and flattened

200g (1 cup) basmati rice

500ml (2 cups) water

100g baby spinach,
    shredded

salt and pepper

Preheat the oven to 200°C/180°C fan/gas 6.

Using a potato peeler, ribbon the cucumber. Add the vinegar, salt and sugar to a bowl with the cucumber and radishes. Set aside to pickle.

Add 1 tablespoon of oil to a heated pan with the onion, ginger, garlic, carrot and apple and cook for 8 minutes until the onion starts to soften and colour. Add 2 tablespoons of flour, the turmeric, curry powder, seasoning, coriander and tomato paste, then cook for 1 minute. Add the honey and stock and stir well for 20 minutes until it thickens. Once thick, blitz with a processor and keep warm.

Add the crumbs to a frying pan with the remaining oil, cook until brown and transfer to a plate. Add the egg to one bowl and remaining flour to another. Take the chicken, dust in flour, then into egg and finally into the crumbs to cover. Bake on a baking tray for 25 minutes, turning after 15 minutes.

Meanwhile, add the rice with double the amount of water to a pan and bring to the boil. Once boiling, cook for 3 minutes, turn off the heat and put a lid on the pan so the rice can carry on steaming for 7–8 minutes. Do not stir as you want the rice to steam, absorb the water and fluff up.

To serve, arrange the rice, sliced chicken and curry sauce with the drained pickles and spinach.

ULTIMATE TUNA JACKETS

Cooking time: 40 minutes
Difficulty: Easy

I was set a challenge with this one as I hate tinned tuna! Instead I'm using tasty tuna steaks along with fragrant pesto, tomato and avocado and finished with just a small hint of heat from the chilli. I promise you'll never have a grey tuna jacket again.

2 jacket potatoes
2 garlic cloves, peeled
juice of 1 lemon
4 tablespoons mayonnaise
25g basil
30g pine nuts, plus extra
    to garnish
2 x 150g tuna steaks
dash of olive oil
1 tablespoon butter
1 avocado, peeled, stoned
    and sliced
2 tomatoes, chopped
¼ red chilli, very finely chopped
salt and pepper

Preheat the oven to 220°C/200°C fan/gas 7.

Cook the potatoes in a microwave on full power for 10 minutes, then place in the oven for 15 minutes, or add the potatoes to the oven for the whole time until soft in the middle.

Take the garlic, lemon juice, mayo, basil, pine nuts and some salt and pepper, place in a blender and blitz until smooth.

Add the tuna steaks to a hot griddle pan with a dash of oil and a little salt and pepper and cook for 3 minutes on each side over a high heat.

Take the tuna steaks and, using a fork, break them up like tinned tuna but more chunky. Add the tuna to the basil mayo pesto and mix together.

Now cross the tops with a knife to open the jacket potatoes. Add the butter and mix into the flesh, then put the avocado and tomato to one side and top with the tuna mix and a sprinkle of the chilli and a scattering of pine nuts.

CHICKEN SHAWARMA & HOMEMADE WRAPS WITH LEMON YOGURT

Cooking time: 25 minutes
Difficulty: Moderate

Who doesn't love a kebab? Especially one wrapped up in a homemade wrap. I spent a month eating these two or three times a week and adding to the recipe to perfect it. It's one of my favourites on a Friday night, so feel free to swap this to a weekend.

1 tablespoon salt

1 tablespoon sugar

50ml white wine vinegar

¼ red cabbage, thinly shredded

50ml cold water

3 chicken breasts

½ red chilli, finely sliced

1 tablespoon honey

2 garlic cloves, crushed

juice and zest of 1 lemon

1 teaspoon cayenne pepper

2 teaspoons cumin powder

1 teaspoon smoked paprika

1 tablespoon vegetable oil

250ml yogurt

3 sprigs of coriander, leaves only

2 tomatoes, sliced

½ cos lettuce, shredded

8 slices of cucumber

salt and pepper

Homemade wraps

90ml hot water

150g light spelt flour, plus extra

50ml olive oil

4 wooden skewers, soaked in
    water for 30 minutes

Add the salt, sugar and vinegar to a bowl with the cabbage, then add water to make sure everything is covered and leave to pickle for 20 minutes.

To make the wraps, mix the hot water, flour and oil together until soft and combined, then dust with flour and leave to rest for 10 minutes.

Meanwhile, slice the chicken across the narrow width into thin slices and add to the skewers. Place on a baking tray, then mix together the chilli, honey, garlic, juice and zest of half the lemon, the cayenne pepper, cumin, paprika, oil and seasoning and baste the skewers. Cook on a hot griddle pan for 20 minutes, turning regularly, until beginning to char all over and cooked through.

Cut the dough into two, then roll each ball out with a rolling pin until you have a nice size wrap. Add each one to a heated frying pan and cook on both sides for 1–2 minutes in total until they puff up.

Mix the yogurt with the remaining lemon juice and a small amount of zest. To serve, add the chicken into the wraps with the drained pickled cabbage, coriander, tomatoes, lettuce and cucumber and finish with a dollop of lemon yogurt. Wrap up in paper and enjoy like a proper kebab!

211

BEEF BULGOGI WITH RICE & SPRING ONIONS

Cooking time: 30 minutes
Marinating time: 2 hours
Difficulty: Easy

The term 'bulgogi' literally means 'fire meat'.
Historically cooked on a griddle or open flame,
I've stripped this back and cooked over a high heat
to replicate that authentic taste. The pear marinade
really is something a bit special in this one.

1 tablespoon honey

2 tablespoons soy sauce

1 pear, peeled, cored
   and halved

1 apple, peeled, cored
   and halved

2 garlic cloves, peeled

½ red chilli

1 teaspoon brown sugar

400g sirloin or rump steak,
   thinly sliced

200g (1 cup) basmati rice

500ml (2 cups) water

1 tablespoon sesame oil

1 carrot, peeled and sliced into
   thin matchsticks

½ onion, peeled and finely sliced

4 spring onions, trimmed and
   sliced on the diagonal

salt and pepper

pear slices, to garnish (optional)

Add the honey, soy sauce, pear, apple, garlic, chilli, sugar and salt and pepper to a blender and blitz, then pour over the steak and stir together. Leave to marinate for 2 hours or overnight (if in a real rush, 30 minutes will do).

When ready to cook, add the rice with double the amount of water to a pan and bring to the boil. Once boiling, cook for 3 minutes, turn off the heat and put a lid on the pan so the rice can carry on steaming for 7–8 minutes. Do not stir as you want the rice to steam, absorb the water and fluff up.

To a deep pan or wok, add the oil and get it nice and hot. Add the beef and stir and flip the meat in the pan, then after the steak starts to brown all over, add the carrot, onion and half the spring onion. Cook for a further minute over a high heat.

Serve with the rice, a few slices of pear, if desired, and a sprinkle of spring onions over the top.

SPAGHETTI ALLA PUTTANESCA

Cooking time: 20 minutes
Difficulty: Easy

Please don't be scared of the anchovies in this dish.
You won't taste them, but they work beautifully to
add a salty flavour that completes this classic sauce.

250g spaghetti

1 tablespoon olive oil

1 garlic clove, peeled
  and crushed

½ onion, peeled and
  finely chopped

½ red chilli, finely sliced

400g tin of chopped tomatoes

4 tinned anchovies

14 black olives

1 tablespoon capers

2 sprigs of basil

30g Parmesan cheese

salt and pepper

Add the spaghetti to a pan of salted boiling water
and cook until starting to soften.

Whilst this is cooking, in a second pan over a
medium heat, add the olive oil, garlic and onion
and start to soften them down, around 4–5 minutes.
Add the chilli and cook for a further minute.

Add the tomatoes and anchovies to a bowl and
mash together, then add this mix to the onion and
continue to cook for 1–2 minutes until the sauce
begins to bubble. Add the olives and capers.

Take the spaghetti out of the water and introduce to
the sauce along with a splash of the pasta cooking
water. Tear in the basil, season and serve with
slithers of Parmesan made using a potato peeler.

BEEF BOURGUIGNON PITHIVIER WITH THYME MASH & SHREDDED GREENS

Cooking time: 1 hour
Cooling time: 40 minutes
Difficulty: Moderate

Bourguignon in a pie, did I hear you say? I mean, what better combination can you get? And finishing this with a herb-infused mash creates an absolute gem of a comfort meal.

---

1 tablespoon olive oil

400g rump steak, sliced

2 bacon rashers, finely chopped

1 onion, peeled and finely sliced

1 garlic clove, crushed

250g chestnut mushrooms, chopped

1 tablespoon tomato paste

1 tablespoon light spelt flour

4 sprigs of thyme, leaves roughly chopped

175ml red wine

3 sprigs of parsley, chopped

220ml beef stock

500g ready-to-roll puff pastry

1 egg, beaten

2 Maris Piper potatoes, peeled and cut into cubes

50g butter

200g cavolo nero, chopped

250ml water

½ tablespoon honey

salt and pepper

Preheat the oven to 200°C/180°C fan/gas 6.

Pour the oil into a heated pan and add the steak, bacon, onion and garlic. Cook for 4–5 minutes until brown. Now add the mushrooms and cook for 2 minutes, then add the tomato paste and cook for a further 30 seconds, lastly add the flour, which will bind to the meat and onions.

Add three chopped sprigs of the thyme and the red wine and mix thoroughly to form a sauce. Add the parsley, beef stock and seasoning and cook for a further 20 minutes until starting to go nice and thick (this could take 5 minutes longer if too runny). Take the mix, add to a bowl and set aside to cool down.

Take the pastry and roll out to around 5mm or the thickness of a £1 coin. Cut out four circles with a medium-sized bowl. Brush the edges of two of the discs with egg and fill with two equal portions of the cooled steak mix (this should be fairly solid and not messy), then take the remaining discs and lay over the top, sealing with the egg wash. Fold the edges up and over all the way around and then make small, curved lines using a sharp knife from the centre outwards on

→

217

Pithivier / continued

top of each pie, but do not cut all the way through or they will leak! Now, using the egg wash, brush the pie tops.

Bake on a baking tray for 25 minutes until the pithiviers are puffed up and golden brown.

Whilst they are cooking, add the potatoes to a pan of salted boiling water and cook until soft. Drain, add the butter and remaining chopped thyme and mash together.

Add the cavolo nero to a saucepan along with the water and honey. Cook over a high heat for 4 minutes with a lid on to steam the greens.

Serve the pastries with the mashed potato and drained steamed greens.

BASKET

10

COMFORTING

IF IT'S A COLD, RAINY WEEK,
THEN SHOP FOR THIS BASKET!
A HOT-AND-SPICY CURRY, WARMING
RAMEN, AND FINISHING OFF WITH
A STUNNING BELLY OF PORK AND
CAULIFLOWER PURÉE. GET A BIT
CHEFFY WITH THE PRESENTATION FOR
THIS ONE – IT'S WORTH THE EFFORT.

MENU FOR THE WEEK AHEAD

MONDAY
Moroccan Beetroot Burgers
& Garlic Wedges

TUESDAY
Speedy Chicken Madras & Turmeric Rice

WEDNESDAY
Crispy Parma Ham & Chives Mac & Cheese

THURSDAY
Spicy Beef Ramen & Soft-Boiled Egg

FRIDAY
Beetroot Crepes with Parma,
Spinach & Cheesy Thyme Mushrooms

SATURDAY
Lemon & Herb Chicken with Green Beans

SUNDAY
Pork Belly, Cauliflower
Purée, Spinach & Glazed Carrots

SHOPPING LIST FOR THE WEEK AHEAD

BASKET

MEAT & FISH
2 chicken breasts
2 chicken breasts, skin on
6 slices of Parma ham
500g rolled pork
　belly joint
400g sirloin steak

DAIRY & EGGS
4 eggs
6 slices of Gruyère
　cheese, plus 20g
605ml milk
15g Parmesan cheese

VEGETABLES
300g baby spinach
270g cooked beetroot
5 carrots, 4 mixed colour
400g small cauliflower
　florets
250g chestnut
　mushrooms
11 garlic cloves
3cm piece of ginger
150g green beans
2 small onions
100g pak choi
1 large potato
3 red chillies
1 red onion
3 handfuls of rocket
2 shallots
6 spring onions

HERBS
8 chives
6 sprigs of coriander
2 sprigs of rosemary
4 sage leaves
7 sprigs of thyme

FRUIT
1 apple
1 lemon
1 lime

GENERAL
400g tin of black beans
3 tablespoons
　breadcrumbs
2 brioche rolls
400g tin of chopped
　tomatoes
20g dried shiitake
　mushrooms
300g egg noodles
140g macaroni
2 tablespoons mirin
160g cooked mixed-
　grain quinoa
3 tablespoons rolled oats
2 tablespoons tomato
　chutney
75ml dry white wine

CUPBOARD

balsamic vinegar
basmati rice
beef stock
brown sugar
butter
chicken stock
chilli powder
cloves
coriander seeds
cumin powder
Dijon mustard
fenugreek seeds
garam masala
honey
light spelt flour
mayonnaise
olive oil
salt and pepper
sea salt
smoked paprika
soy sauce
turmeric
vegetable oil

MOROCCAN BEETROOT BURGERS & GARLIC WEDGES

Cooking time: 45 minutes
Difficulty: Hard

Possibly the best vegetarian burger you'll ever make! Yes, it's a bold statement, but one I'll stand by. This one even stands up to being barbecued without falling apart like so many others do. These also batch freeze really well, to be cooked later.

1 teaspoon olive oil, plus extra
    for cooking the wedges
    and burgers
½ red onion, peeled and
    finely chopped
3 garlic cloves, peeled,
    1 crushed and 2 chopped
1 teaspoon cumin powder
½ teaspoon smoked paprika
200g cooked beetroot, drained
400g tin of black beans, drained
160g cooked mixed-grain quinoa
1 egg
3 tablespoons breadcrumbs
3 tablespoons rolled oats, blitzed
    to a flour in a blender
1 large potato, cut into wedges
2 sprigs of rosemary,
    finely chopped
2 brioche rolls
1 tablespoon mayonnaise
2 tablespoons tomato chutney
2 slices of Gruyère cheese
8–10 baby spinach leaves
salt and pepper

Preheat the oven to 220°C/200°C fan/gas 7.

Add the oil to a hot pan with the onion and crushed garlic and cook for 2–3 minutes until starting to soften. Add the spices and cook for 1 minute.

Take a blender, add the beetroot and blitz for 5 seconds only as you don't want this to go mushy, then add the beans and blitz again for 10 seconds. Tip into a bowl, add the onion mix, salt, pepper, the quinoa, egg and breadcrumbs and stir together.

Slowly mix the oat flour into the burger mix, adding a little at a time to get the right consistency for shaping by hand. Form into two small patties and allow to cool in the fridge to firm up.

Cook the wedges, a drizzle of oil, the rosemary and chopped garlic in a roasting tray for 20–25 minutes.

In an oiled griddle pan over a medium heat, cook the burgers for 8 minutes, turning regularly. Finish off in the oven with the wedges for 3–4 minutes.

Toast the brioche rolls, add a scoop of mayo to each bottom half, then the tomato chutney and burger and top with the cheese and spinach. Serve with the wedges on the side.

SPEEDY CHICKEN MADRAS & TURMERIC RICE

Cooking time: 40 minutes
Difficulty: Moderate

This one's a spicy one, so add as little or as much chilli powder as you want. For me, the madras has to have a kick!

1 teaspoon vegetable oil,
  plus extra for the rice
2 small onions, peeled and
  1 finely sliced, 1 finely chopped
1cm piece of ginger, peeled
  and grated
2 garlic cloves, crushed
1 carrot, peeled and finely chopped
1 teaspoon cumin powder
3 teaspoons turmeric
1 teaspoon chilli powder
  (optional)
2 red chillies, finely chopped
1 teaspoon coriander
  seeds, crushed
1 teaspoon fenugreek
  seeds, crushed
1 teaspoon garam masala
400g tin of chopped tomatoes
2 chicken breasts, cut into cubes
1 clove
200g (1 cup) basmati rice
500ml (2 cups) water
3 sprigs of coriander, leaves only
salt and pepper

Add the oil to a heated pan with the sliced onion, ginger and garlic and cook for 3 minutes over a medium heat. Add the carrot, cumin, half the turmeric, the chilli powder, if using, chillies, coriander and fenugreek seeds, garam masala and a little seasoning and cook for 3 minutes. Add the tomatoes, bring the sauce up to a bubbling heat, then blitz the sauce with a blender.

Put the sauce back over the heat, add the chicken and simmer for 15 minutes until the chicken is cooked through and piping hot in the centre.

Meanwhile, add the chopped onion to a little vegetable oil in a separate pan and cook until translucent and softened. Add the clove, the remaining turmeric and the rice to the pan with double the quantity of water to rice. Stir the rice to make sure the onion is well mixed in, then bring to the boil, add a lid and turn to a low temperature for around 7 minutes or until the water has been absorbed.

Serve the rice with a scoop of curry and garnished with the coriander.

CRISPY PARMA HAM & CHIVES MAC & CHEESE

Cooking time: 45 minutes
Difficulty: Easy

This indulgent twist on a classic is packed full of flavour. The combination of Gruyère cheese and the crispy saltiness of the Parma ham really makes this dish special.

140g macaroni

1 teaspoon olive oil

¼ red onion, peeled and
    finely sliced

1 garlic clove, peeled and crushed

1 sprig of thyme

300ml milk

1 teaspoon Dijon mustard

4 slices of Parma ham

30g butter

25g light spelt flour

20g Gruyère cheese, grated

8 chives, finely chopped

15g Parmesan cheese,
    finely grated

salt and pepper

Preheat the oven to 220°C/200°C fan/gas 7.

Cook the macaroni in a pan of salted boiling water until beginning to soften, then drain and set aside (you can drizzle with oil if you want it to be loose and not too sticky).

Heat the oil in a saucepan over a medium heat, add the onion, garlic and thyme and cook until the onion is soft. Add the milk and mustard and bring up to a warm temperature.

Lay the Parma ham on a baking tray and grill on full heat for around 8 minutes until crispy and golden, turning regularly.

Add the butter and flour in a second pan, and mix together over a low heat until combined and smooth. Slowly add the milk mixture to the flour, a little at a time, mixing really fast with a whisk. Once you have a smooth consistency, add the macaroni, then the Gruyère with a pinch of seasoning and mix in so that the cheese becomes stringy. Add the chives and crumble or break the crispy Parma ham into the mix, stirring thoroughly.

Add the mac and cheese to two small ovenproof serving dishes, top with the Parmesan and bake for 20 minutes until golden brown on top.

SPICY BEEF RAMEN & SOFT-BOILED EGG

Cooking time: 30 minutes
Difficulty: Easy

You can go into real depth with ramens and the stocks used can take days to make. I've tried to simplify this classic dish to have it in front of you, ready to slurp the noodles down, within 30 minutes.

20g dried shiitake mushrooms

1 litre beef stock

2 tablespoons soy sauce

2 tablespoons mirin

2 garlic cloves, peeled and crushed

2cm piece of ginger,
    peeled and grated

1 teaspoon brown sugar

juice of ½ lime

400g sirloin steak

1 teaspoon vegetable oil

100g pak choi, quartered

2 eggs

300g egg noodles

1 red chilli, finely chopped

3 sprigs of coriander,
    finely chopped

2 spring onions, trimmed and
    sliced on the diagonal

salt and pepper

Add the shiitakes to the stock in a pan and bring to a light bubble, then add the soy, mirin, garlic and ginger. Whilst this is simmering, the mushrooms will be infusing the stock with flavour. Add the sugar, lime juice and half lime to the broth, adding more water if the broth starts to evaporate too quickly. It's best to try and get all three pans cooking with this one – broth, steak and eggs – to ensure you have lots of broth at the end.

Meanwhile, season the steak, rub in a little oil and add to a piping hot pan or griddle. Cook over a high heat for 3–4 minutes each side for medium-rare (which works well with this dish) or add another 30 seconds each side for medium. Leave the steak to rest and put the pak choi on the griddle pan to soak up some of the beefy flavours and create char lines. Add a tiny splash of water to the pan to give a little steam to the cabbage before starting to char again. After cooking for 2 minutes, add to the steak.

Put the eggs in a pan of boiling water and cook for exactly 6 minutes. Meanwhile, add the noodles to the broth and cook until softening. Pop the cooked eggs into cold water, then peel and slice in half.

Add the noodles to two bowls, layer with the broth, top with the pak choi, then finely slice the steak and layer this into both bowls along with the soft-boiled egg. Scatter with the finely chopped chilli, coriander and spring onion.

BEETROOT CREPES WITH PARMA, SPINACH & CHEESY THYME MUSHROOMS

Cooking time: 30 minutes
Difficulty: Moderate

This was created whilst testing brunch ideas using different batters. The vibrancy from the beetroot looks (and tastes!) incredible in the crepes. Paired with the cheesy, spinach goodness, you have the ultimate wrap.

170g light spelt flour

230ml milk

1 egg

70g cooked beetroot, drained
    and sliced

2 tablespoons olive oil

250g chestnut mushrooms, sliced

½ garlic clove, crushed

2 sprigs of thyme

1 teaspoon balsamic vinegar

2 slices of Parma ham

4 slices of Gruyère cheese

10 baby spinach leaves

1 handful of rocket, plus
    extra to serve

salt and pepper

Add the flour, milk, egg, a pinch of salt and the beetroot to a blender and blitz until smooth.

Add a little of the oil to a hot frying pan with the mushrooms and garlic, cook for 1 minute, then add the sprigs of thyme by dragging your fingers down each sprig to release the leaves. Pour in a splash of balsamic vinegar and a pinch of salt and pepper and cook over a high heat to get colour onto the mushrooms. Add these to a bowl and set aside.

Now add the Parma ham to the pan and cook until crisp, around 1–2 minutes in a super-hot pan! Again, set the cooked Parma ham to one side.

Add a small amount of the remaining oil to the pan, then pour one to two ladles of the crepe batter into the centre of the pan and swirl to make the crepe fill out to the surrounding area of the pan. Cook for 40 seconds over a high heat, then flip or turn over with a spatula. Cook for another minute until starting to brown, then add half the mushrooms and half the Parma ham and Gruyère.

Place under a hot grill for 1 minute to bubble up and melt the cheese. Lay half the spinach down the centre aligned with a scattering of rocket, fold over and serve. Repeat to make your second crepe.

239

LEMON & HERB CHICKEN WITH GREEN BEANS

Cooking time: 35 minutes
Difficulty: Easy

This recipe crisps up the chicken skin until deeply golden, before braising to really permeate the meat with the flavours of lemon and thyme. This is a light dish, so feel free to add a roasted sweet potato.

1 tablespoon olive oil
2 chicken breasts, skin on
2 shallots, peeled and
   halved lengthways
1 garlic clove, crushed
10g butter
1 tablespoon honey
2 sprigs of thyme
1 lemon, sliced into 4 slices
75ml dry white wine
150ml chicken stock
150g green beans, trimmed
salt

In a non-stick deep saucepan, heat the oil over a medium heat. Pat dry the chicken skin and season with salt. Add the chicken to the pan, skin-side down, and slowly cook for 8–10 minutes until the skin is deeply golden and crisp. Remove and set aside.

Add the shallot halves to the pan and colour until golden. Remove and set aside.

Add the garlic, butter, honey, thyme and lemon slices to the pan and cook for 2 minutes. Return the chicken to the pan, skin-side up, and add the wine, chicken stock and shallots, taking care not to get liquid on the chicken skin.

Turn the heat down low and simmer for 15 minutes until the chicken is cooked, the shallots are tender and the sauce is reduced.

Meanwhile, cook the green beans in a separate pan of salted boiling water until just tender, then drain. Serve the chicken with the green beans.

PORK BELLY, CAULIFLOWER PURÉE, SPINACH & GLAZED CARROTS

Cooking time: 1 hour 15 minutes
Difficulty: Hard

This simple, but delicious dish was created for my friends in South Africa, who absolutely love pork belly with crackling. I hope you love it too.

---

1 apple, cored and sliced
   into thick chunks
2 tablespoons honey
4 sage leaves
2 garlic cloves, crushed
2 tablespoons olive oil
500g rolled pork belly joint
4 mixed coloured carrots
400g small cauliflower florets
20g butter
2 sprigs of thyme
75ml milk
4 spring onions, trimmed
200g baby spinach
salt and pepper
sea salt

Preheat the oven to 160°C/140°C fan/gas 3.

Add the apple, 1 tablespoon of the honey, the sage, garlic and a tablespoon of olive oil to a roasting tin and lay the pork on top, skin-side up. Dry the pork skin and then score the top, adding a generous amount of salt. Roast for 1 hour.

After the pork has been roasting for 45 minutes, add the carrots to a second tin, season and drizzle with a little of the remaining olive oil and honey, then roast for about 30 minutes or until caramelised.

Add the cauliflower to a pan of salted boiling water and cook for 3 minutes until soft. Drain, then add the butter, thyme and some of the milk, season and blitz in a food processor until silky smooth. If needed, add more milk a little at a time, to loosen the consistency.

Take the pork from the oven and place under a hot grill for 5–7 minutes along with the spring onions. Cook until the pork crackling begins to bubble up. Remove and rest for 10 minutes while the carrots finish cooking.

Cook the spinach in a lightly oiled and seasoned pan for 1 minute until just wilted. Serve the sliced pork on a swirl of cauliflower purée with the spring onions, carrots and spinach. Season and drizzle with juices from the roasting tin.

INDEX

ACKNOWLEDGEMENTS

I'd like to thank each and every one of you who has helped take this book from an idea to reality over the past year and to those who have shared my passion to make *The 7-Day Basket* a book available for everyone to use. You've all believed in my concept and I truly feel it will change the way people shop and cook.

To all the people who have followed my social media journey and seen it grow as a small, friendly community, your support via my social channels make these opportunities happen, and listening to what you wanted in a book has made *The 7-Day Basket* come to life. I've listened to you all, from recipe ideas to your firm favourites.

A huge thanks to my wife, who, no matter what, along with my mother-in-law, Judy, tirelessly tested each of my recipes to make sure they tasted good. I always found it so convenient that you'd both be at home on food test days. Jokes aside, I simply couldn't have done this without my family's support from start to finish.

A huge thanks to my wonderful Headline Home family. I truly believe we were all put together to make this book everything it has become, from beautifully styled food with the hugely talented Emma Lahaye and Rosie Mackean, to outstanding photography and also patience from Al Richardson, not to mention design from Charlotte Heal and Tegan Hendel and editing from Kay Halsey.

I also cannot thank Lindsey Evans and Kate Miles enough for, firstly, putting the team together and, lastly, making everything run so smoothly from start to finish (oh, and a shout out for Kate's hard work stepping in on lighting duties for the entire food shoot! Without you, Al would have been working in the dark).

A huge thanks to Jessica Farrugia for her PR work, which I'm sure I'll be thanking you for months to come, and to Rob Chilver in marketing.

Lastly, a massive shout out to my Gleam management, who have got this idea out to the world and backed me from the beginning. Thank you Jess, Fran, Lily, Lauren, Abigail, Megan, Dom and all the others who have been involved along the way.

First published in Great Britain in 2019
by Headline Home
an imprint of Headline Publishing Group

1

Cataloguing in Publication Data is available from the British Library

Hardback ISBN 978 1 4722 6363 6
eISBN 978 1 4722 6362 9

Commissioning Editor: Lindsey Evans
Senior Editor: Kate Miles
Design: Charlotte Heal Design
Food and Prop Styling: Emma LaHaye
Food Styling Assistant: Rosie Mackean
Copy Editor: Kay Halsey
Proofreaders: Anne Sheasby and Anna Herve
Indexer: Caroline Wilding

Printed and bound in Italy by L.E.G.O. S.p.A.
Colour reproduction by Alta Image, London

HEADLINE PUBLISHING GROUP
An Hachette UK Company
Carmelite House
50 Victoria Embankment
London EC4Y 0DZ

www.headline.co.uk
www.hachette.co.uk